FeARLESS WRItIN G

Multigenre
to Motivate
and Inspire

Tom Romano

HEINEMANN
Portsmouth, NH

Heinemann
361 Hanover Street
Portsmouth, NH 03801–3912
www.heinemann.com

Offices and agents throughout the world

The author and publisher wish to thank those who have generously given permission to reprint borrowed material:

Excerpt from "Teacher-Student Conferencing: A Way to Writing Improvement" by Tom Romano. Originally appeared in the *English Language Arts Bulletin*, Winter/Spring 1982 (vol. 23, pp. 6-19). Reprinted by permission of the *Ohio Journal of English Language Arts*.

Excerpt from "If You Talk in Your Sleep" written by Johnny Christopher and Bobby "Red" West. Used by permission of Elvis Music Inc., c/o Carlin America, Inc.

Excerpts from "At the Cancer Clinic" by Ted Kooser from *Delights & Shadows*. Copyright © 2004 by Ted Kooser. Reprinted with the permission of The Permissions Company, Inc. on behalf of Copper Canyon Press, www.coppercanyonpress.org.

"Waiting for the Dog" from *Whale Song: A Poet's Journey into Cancer* by Kenneth W. Brewer. Copyright © 2013 by Dream Garden Press and the estate of Kenneth Brewer. Reprinted by permission. All rights reserved.

Excerpts from Chapter 19 originally appeared in "Teaching Writing from the Inside" by Tom Romano from *Adolescent Literacy* by Kylene Beers, Robert E. Probst, and Linda Rief. Copyright © 2007 by Kylene Beers, Robert E. Probst, and Linda Rief. Published by Heinemann, Portsmouth, NH. All rights reserved.

"The Truth About Why I Love Potatoes" by Mekeel McBride from *Dog Star Delicatessen: New and Selected Poems 1979-2006*. Copyright © 2001 by Mekeel McBride. Reprinted by permission of The Permissions Company, Inc., on behalf of Carnegie Mellon University Press, www.cmu.edu/universitypress.

"To My Colleagues in the Field" by Tom Romano from *College Composition and Communication* (vol. 41, no. 4, December 1990). Reprinted by permission of the National Council of Teachers of English.

Excerpts from Sections I, II, IV, and V originally appeared in "The Many Ways of Multigenre" by Tom Romano from *Teaching the Neglected "R"* by Tom Newkirk and Richard Kent, editors. Copyright © 2007 by Tom Newkirk and Richard Kent. Published by Heinemann, Portsmouth, NH. All rights reserved.

Excerpts from the *Common Core State Standards* © Copyright 2010. National Governors Association Center for Best Practices and Council of Chief State School Officers. All rights reserved

Library of Congress Cataloging-in-Publication Data

Romano, Tom.
  Fearless writing : multigenre to motivate and inspire / Tom Romano.
    pages cm
  Includes bibliographical references.
  ISBN 978-0-325-04806-2
  1. Language arts (Middle school)—United States. 2. Language arts (Secondary)—
United States. 3. English language—Rhetoric—Study and teaching. 4. Report writing—
Study and teaching. 5. English language—Style. 6. Literary form. I. Title.

  LB1631.R593 2013
  428.0071'2—dc23   2013009193

Editor: Tobey Antao
Production: Hilary Zusman
Cover design: Judy Arisman
Interior design: Shawn Girsberger
Typesetter: Shawn Girsberger
Manufacturing: Steve Bernier

Printed in the United States of America on acid-free paper

17 16 15 14 13 VP 1 2 3 4 5

FOR the GiRLS:

Kathy, Mariana, Leah Mae, Anna Kate,

a multigenre foursome to reckon with

contents

I am large, I contain multitudes

WALT WHITMAN

Origins, Definitions, Sample Multigenre Paper

When ideas come in a flash of insight, more often than not they actually didn't. They arrived as the result of rich history, periods of gestation, and alertness to possibility. I also pay attention to bellwethers, those students with irrepressible voices and a willingness to risk. They accomplish what we never thought to ask for but wish we had.

1

Personal History

A Shift in the Territory

FIRST, A STORY FROM DEEP INTO MY TEACHING LIFE:

Mid-May, 1988. Not much school left. Not many more written words by 150 teenagers. It's evening. My daughter, home from track practice, has commandeered the family room. She eats leftover broccoli and cheese casserole, talks on the telephone, keeps an eye on a television sitcom, and somewhere amid all that does homework.

One room away I sit at my desk, a glass of red wine within reach, a stack of research papers near. I am undaunted. These papers are the fruition of a new research assignment I've tried with high school seniors. Instead of producing expository papers, students are writing in many genres. Although each piece is self-contained, making a point of its own, taken together, all the writing creates a unified whole. I call the assignment a "multigenre research paper."

I reach for Brian's. What a great kid. School plays, musicals, chorus—a delightful young man who combines intellect, wit, and irresistible charm. Students from every clique in school like Brian. Teachers, too, from the chemistry lab to the art room. Brian has written his multigenre research paper about John Lennon, his musical-social-political hero who was murdered in 1980, when Brian was nine years old. He's titled the paper "The Long and Wonderful Odyssey of the Walrus—A Heart Play." I turn to the first piece of writing (Romano 1995, 122):

Unfinished Music #1—John

He hit the pavement
ass-first
Yoko raised
his
head.
He wanted to embrace her

but a hundred people
were
standing on
his arms.
　　Oh, God, Yoko, I've been shot

I stop sipping wine. I hear neither the sitcom's laugh track nor my daughter's occasional outbursts of personality. I am rapt, immersed in a world of fact, imagination, and creativity—all this woven together by a high school kid. I am a progressive English teacher with sixteen years' experience, a master's degree in English Education, and an active professional life as an associate of the Ohio Writing Project. Still, during these weeks in May when students show me what can be done with multigenre, I sense my teaching, my very career, shifting forever.

CHapTer 2

Why Read *Fearless Writing*?

IT WILL ROUSE YOUR PASSION FOR EXCELLENT WRITING.

You will resonate to many written voices singing their songs.

You will think. You will question. You will learn.

I can't guarantee that multigenre will alter your career as it did mine. I'm not even sure that's a good idea. You are, no doubt, leading students to engage in productive, challenging composing. I do believe, however, that multigenre will expand your notion of writing and teaching writing. You'll awaken to different ways that students may communicate their learning. And I'm counting on this: reading my ideas about teaching writing will spur your own.

You won't find multigenre mentioned in the Common Core Standards for writing. That doesn't surprise me, given the Common Core's veiled dismissal of any writing that smacks of creativity and imagination. Even so, through multigenre, students can meet many writing standards demanded in the Common Core. Multigenre doesn't have to be an add-on. Imperative skills and concepts can be woven naturally into it—text types, research skills, rhetorical strategies, voice, point of view, grammar, usage, punctuation, genre study, expressive writing to launch all writing, revision, and the reading of wide-ranging nonfiction texts as writers hungrily pursue their research interests.

In the twenty-five years I've taught multigenre, I've seen it spread across the land. I've seen Kentucky Educational Television produce a series of eight videos about teaching writing in middle school, one of which is devoted exclusively to multigenre (KET 2004). To my classroom one summer at the University of New Hampshire, I welcomed Barry Lane, that itinerant troubadour of teaching writing. Barry shot brief video of me explaining multigenre. That evening I saw it on YouTube complete with titles and music (Lane 2009). I've had teachers elementary school through college tell me how multigenre has transformed their teaching. I've had students tell me of the power of multigenre, like Daniel, one of my college students:

Creating a multigenre paper was like having the handcuffs taken off my writing. At first I had no idea what to do, but as I began writing, the paper seemed to shape itself. I was able to write in new styles that I've always been interested in but never tried. This paper helped me to grow as a writer because it allowed me to be expressive, take risks, and share my opinion.

Multigenre has caught on, I believe, because students and teachers find it motivating and inspiring. I've found it most effective to lead students into multigenre writing near the end of a semester or year. By that time students have renewed their acquaintance with a number of genres through their reading and writing. Multigenre is the opportunity to synthesize their genre savvy. And nothing I know of has worked better at rekindling students' academic energy and keeping end-of-year writing doldrums at bay.

The question might arise, though: Is multigenre fluff? Is it serious intellectual work? Isn't writing analytically about someone else's creation really what counts as being academically rigorous? You'll have to decide where you stand on that. As a reader, writer, and teacher I know where I stand. I've read literature since I was a child. I've devoted my life to teaching English language arts. I believe that writing a novel, play, poem, or creative nonfiction is a rigorous activity that melds intellect and emotion, fact and imagination, design and spontaneity.

Multigenre research writing shows faith in students as meaning makers who participate in creating the big world mural of writing. It isn't just literary royalty that gets to write something other than analytical essays—not just Dickens and Kingsolver, Keats and Kooser, Shakespeare and Ephron, Dafoe and Lamott. It's Holly and Carmon, too. Mark and Marina. Eduardo and Darius. Multigenre is democratic, inclusive, and creative (as all writing is when we approach it as writers who use language as the creative medium).

I've divided *Fearless Writing* into five sections:

In Section I, which you're amidst right now, I tell you some of the interesting history of multigenre in our literary heritage. At the end of this section I include a complete multigenre paper by one of my students. You can also go to www.users.muohio.edu/romanots and read a dozen more multigenre papers by my college students.

In Section II, I share how I've learned to prepare students to write multigenre papers, setting up assignments that urge them to explore, plan, and expand their thinking. Although I welcome inspiration in my own writing, I don't wait for it to strike. I don't let my students wait either. I jump-start their thinking, which leads them to further writing, further genres, further discovery.

In Section III, I describe genres and subgenres students might try that can form the core of their multigenre papers. This section comprises nearly a third of the book. Practical ideas abound.

In Section IV, I alert you to three components I've found critical to creating successful multigenre papers: beginnings, golden threads, and endnotes.

In Section V, I discuss how I grade multigenre papers. If you know my previous work, you might raise your eyebrows to learn I've created a rubric I hope keeps me thorough, rigorous, fair, and appreciative. I've also written two chapters about multigenre's fit with the Common Core Standards for writing.

Last night on public television's "Great Performances" I watched the Beatles' *Magical Mystery Tour*. Although many know the album, fewer know the film created by and starring the "Fab Four," as the group was called at the beginning of the British rock-'n'-roll invasion that featured hermits, animals, dreamers, searchers, stones, zombies, and troggs. Although British television viewers saw the *Magical Mystery Tour* once, in December 1967, American viewers had never seen it.

Every book I've written has been a kind of magical mystery tour. There were stretches when I was absolutely sure of the journey ahead. There were setbacks, doubts, and dead ends too, times when I was stymied, wondering which way to go. There were breakthroughs, surprises of language and insight. There was the quiet exhilaration of surging to the finish.

Hemingway said that "easy writing makes hard reading." I'm a believer in that. My early draft—usually overwritten here, underwritten there, and off the mark—only hints at my final thinking several revisions later. I do what it takes to get there. I wouldn't call my writing process hard. But it requires work, work I find fulfilling. Every failure I discover in diction, syntax, rhythm, and meaning leads to success as I tinker, revise, and polish. If I've done my job, your reading of *Fearless Writing* will be easy. I hope it's also rewarding.

3

Definition
of
Multigenre

FOR READERS WHO HAVE NEVER EXPERIENCED A MULTIGENRE paper, a formal definition is in order:

A multigenre paper arises from research, experience, and imagination. It is not an uninterrupted, expository monolog nor a seamless narrative. A multigenre paper is composed of many genres and subgenres, each piece self-contained, making a point of its own, yet connected to other pieces by theme and content and sometimes by repeated language, images, and genres. A multigenre paper may also contain many voices, not just the author's. The craft then—the challenge for the writer—is to make such a paper hang together as one unified whole.

Some Multigenre History

Dialog with a Skeptic

Skeptic: Hold on!

Romano: Yes? You look concerned.

Skeptic: I am concerned. Multigenre has no thesis statement.

Romano: There can be a thesis statement. It isn't required.

Skeptic: How does the reader know what's being argued? The writer will be all over the lot.

Romano: You read novels, don't you?

Skeptic: Of course.

Romano: And poetry.

Skeptic: Yes, I see myself primarily as a literature teacher.

Romano: You never complain about novels and poetry not having thesis statements.

Skeptic: That's different. That's literature.

Romano: I know. Literature is often "emphatically implicit."

Skeptic: That's an oxymoron.

Romano: Maybe, but I stand by "emphatically implicit." A third-grade boy shouts that a schnauzer looks like "an old grandpa lookin' dog."

Skeptic: So?

Romano: That's emphatically implicit, too. He doesn't say that a grandpa can have bushy eyebrows, a beard, and maybe a grumpy expression, but those possibilities are contained in the metaphor.

Skeptic: OK, I'll grant you that metaphorical language is emphatically implicit, but we're talking about an academic paper.

Romano: *Academic* doesn't have to be narrowly defined. Multigenre research papers call upon writers to *render* experience, just as authors of fiction, poetry, and creative nonfiction do.

Skeptic: Wait a minute. Your definition of multigenre contains both research *and* imagination?

Romano: That's right.

Skeptic: There I have a problem.

Romano: You do?

Skeptic: Come on! If you're doing research, you don't make things up!

Romano: Flannery O'Conner said that imagination is a form of knowledge (quoted in Murray 1990).

Skeptic: She was a fiction writer.

Romano: Albert Einstein wasn't.

Skeptic: So?

Romano: Einstein was the quintessential scientist and mathematician. He was reason and calculation without emotion, yet he understood imagination's powerful role in knowing and learning. "Imagination," he said, "is more important than knowledge" (Moncur 2006).

Skeptic: I do remember Einstein describing how he came to the theory of relativity by imagining himself in space riding on a light wave.

Romano: Yes, he was immersed in a topic. His right brain went to work, unbidden, and imagined a surreal image that led to insight.

Skeptic: OK, so it's not just artistic types who can use imagination.

Romano: Right. Everyone can. Human beings have the capacity to imagine.

Skeptic: It's just that imagination makes me think of whimsy, make believe, the fantastical.

Romano: Imagination is home to the fantastical, too. And I see that gives you pause.

Skeptic: When I think of students writing in academia, I don't think of this multigenre writing you're talking about.

Romano: Understandable. Our default thinking about writing in school is thesis, argument, elucidation, claim, warrant, logical movement of the mind.

Skeptic: That's more like it.

Romano: I value those qualities. I want them in my own writing. I want them in my students' writing. But I also want synthesis. And I want room for imagination.

Skeptic: I see how imagination works with analysis and synthesis. That's what Einstein was doing when he rode that light wave like a bronc.

Romano: Let me cite one more quote about imagination. This one from the philosopher, Immanuel Kant: "The imagination is a necessary ingredient of perception itself" (quoted in Lehrer 2007, 116).

Skeptic: That certainly holds true with Einstein perceiving the theory of relativity.

Romano: When we imagine, we see more deeply, we entertain possibilities we hadn't considered. Some people, for example, are able to deeply imagine what someone else is feeling. I have a neighbor who's good at that. He has great empathy, which comes out of his own troubled childhood. He's able to vividly imagine the experience of others and how that might affect them.

Skeptic: Where did this multigenre idea come from anyway? A state education department? A federal education mandate, something like the Common Core Standards?

Romano: Hardly. The idea for multigenre came from passion.

Skeptic: There's room for passion in educational policy?

Romano: I wouldn't be a teacher if I didn't think so. I'm talking about literate passion. Teachers pursuing their passions in reading and writing. In a bookstore in Stratford, Ontario, one summer, I took a volume from the shelf solely because of its title: *The Collected Works of Billy the Kid* by Michael Ondaatje (1970).

Skeptic: Billy the Kid was a writer *and* an outlaw?

Romano: Only thing I can figure is that "collected works" refers to the way in which Ondaatje wrote about this mythic character of the American west.

Skeptic: You sure it's not a biography?

Romano: I wouldn't call it biography, though it's clearly based upon facts about Billy the Kid and the events in Lincoln County, New Mexico, circa 1880.

Skeptic: Ondaatje used imagination to write the book?

Romano: Yes.

Skeptic: Maybe it's historical fiction.

Romano: I wouldn't call it that.

Skeptic: Is it poetry?

Romano: Some of it is.

Skeptic: Sounds like multiple genres.

Romano: Exactly. Ondaatje rendered events in Billy the Kid's life and the Lincoln County War through narrative vignettes, tangential short stories, character sketches, anecdotes, poems, prose poems, a bawdy song, dialog exchanges, an invented newspaper interview, fragmented scenes repeated from different angles, even quotations from historical figures that Ondaatje fashioned into found poems.

Skeptic: I see where you got the term *multigenre*.

Romano: Multivoice, too. Sometimes you aren't sure which character is speaking or who is being written about.

Skeptic: Sounds postmodern.

Romano: Or maddening. The intriguing thing for me, though, is how Ondaatje uses imagination to render scenes that *might* have taken place.

Skeptic: Like Einstein riding that light wave.

Romano: Late in the book you encounter a poem that occurs while Billy the Kid is dying.

Skeptic: So Ondaatje envisioned that scene from historical accounts.

Romano: Not exactly. Through all the genres you come to know the complexity of Billy the Kid, not just the cold bloodedness. Ondaatje takes you inside the Kid, dramatically, in the last seconds of his life.

Skeptic: How so?

Romano: The speaker of the poem is Billy.

Skeptic: Billy the Kid was an historical character, not a fictional one. Ondaatje can't know what he was thinking when he died. No one can.

Romano: An omniscient author can. And that's what Ondaatje does: he imagines through first person the experience of Billy's dying, including physical details of the scene as well as images and motifs from earlier in the book.

Skeptic: Things that might flash through someone's dying mind.

Romano: I think so.

Skeptic: Your explanation of multigenre has me thinking of a classic American movie.

Romano: What's that?

Skeptic: *On the Waterfront* (1954).

Romano: I love that film. What's its connection to multigenre?

Skeptic: In the most famous scene Terry Malloy, the ex-prizefighter played by Marlon Brando, sits in the backseat of a taxicab with his older brother, Charlie, a corrupt union lawyer played by Rod Steiger. Charlie is in the hip pocket of the mob that controls the union and terrorizes the longshoremen.

Romano: He's a puppet.

Skeptic: And Terry's having problems. He's learned about corruption and murder in the union. His conscience has awakened. He's thinking about telling the federal crime commission what he knows.

Romano: And Charlie can't let that happen.

Skeptic: Right. He's been instructed by the mob to either get Terry to keep his mouth shut or kill him.

Romano: Or he'll be murdered himself.

Skeptic: So Charlie's exasperated. He shouts at Terry, "Are you in or out?" And Terry says, "There's more to this than I thought."

Romano: I see the connection!

Skeptic: There's more to multigenre than I originally thought.

Romano: There is indeed.

Skeptic: One thing I want to ask you.

Romano: Yes?

Skeptic: The definition of multigenre in the previous chapter—
that's pretty straight expository writing.

Romano: Nothing wrong with that.

Skeptic: It's just that I expected more from Mr. Multigenre.

Romano: Next chapter.

5

Definition of Multigenre in the Spirit of Multigenre

I am what I am.

I am imagination and metaphor. I am images
that make you see and wonder and speculate.

I am the enigmatic final line of a poem you carry for days.

I am what I am.

I resist exposition, though I am not averse to it.

I am opposition to a strict writing diet
of thesis-driven, five-paragraph-you-know-whats.

I am what I am.

I am the lash in the eye of tradition.

I am not thesis, though I am pointed.

I am "not necessarily" to those who demand everything be
explained.

I am a force against the prosaic
(and that does not mean writing in prose).

I am what I am.

I am emphatically implicit, the high wire act without a net.

I am, as Whitman wrote, "Expecting the main things from you."

I am what I am.

I am not above falling on my face.

I am Pandora's Rhetorical Box.

I am one and I am many.

I am many and I am one.

I am not mashed potatoes. I am cioppino.

I am trust me, travel with me, be patient.

I am telling you by showing you.

I am multigenre.

What's Wrong with Exposition?

(Well-Written, Pointed, Voiceful Exposition, of Course)

WHAT'S WRONG WITH EXPOSITION? NOTHING. BUT EXPOSITORY writing is not the only genre in town.

My department's webpage has links to thumbnail bios and photos of faculty and staff. At the end of my bio, I listed two non-negotiables of my teaching: (1) "He reads a poem at the beginning of every class" and (2) "His students write in different genres, not merely expository essays."

A colleague objected to my use of *merely*. He said that it demeaned expository writing. My colleague works hard to get students to write fully supported arguments. When it comes to student writing, he's all about claim and warrant and elaboration. Expository writing, he maintains, the crucible of composition, is *rigor* in learning to write.

His objection gave me pause. I think he's right about my choice of adverb. *Merely* disses expository writing. I don't intend that. The bulk of my writing is expository. I don't mean to bite the genre that feeds me. I know, though, that all expository writing is not created equal. The brand of exposition I strive to write is readable as well as informative and persuasive. I believe in varying sentence lengths to avoid sameness and emphasize what's important. I believe in making paragraphs not just to organize my points but also to give readers breaks from unrelenting blocks of text. I believe in finding the strongest verbs I can ("verbs of muscle," Mary Oliver calls them [1995, 89]). I believe in limiting adverbs and finding adjectives of "exactitude" (Oliver 1995, 89). I seek to tuck into my prose surprises of thinking, perception, and language.

Most importantly, I believe in using story and anecdote. I seek to *people* my writing, to make concrete the abstract thoughts I'm arguing/conveying/explaining. I've been doing this for years, ever since reading Ken Macrorie (1976). Recently, I've read Thomas Newkirk's *The Art of Slow Reading: Six Time-Honored Practices for Engagement* (2011). In a chapter about expository writing, Newkirk succinctly articulates what I feel:

[E]xpository writers must also be able to create the sense of presence, of being there, if their ideas are to be convincing and even understood (even remembered). Exposition that is unleavened by description and narration is almost intolerable to read. (2011, 185)

Still, there in my bio on the department home page was a subconscious disdain for expository writing, manifested in that adverb. Where did *merely* come from? I think I know. Expository writing monopolizes thinking in education. As students move through school, they write fewer and fewer poems, metaphors, images, stories, and narratives. Exposition becomes their sole writing diet: reports of various kinds, summaries, essay exams, traditional research papers.

I oppose such exclusivity. Writing is a big world mural, not a snapshot. Writing is book reviews, email messages, notebook entries, news stories, love notes, commentaries, technical instructions, poems of many kinds, so many genres and subgenres that assembling a comprehensive list of them will almost certainly be incomplete. Although I remain steadfast in my opposition to genre monopoly, my expository colleague will be glad to know that on my thumbnail faculty biography I changed *merely* to *only*.

I don't want students—kindergarten through postgraduate school—to become Johnny-One-Genres, which is what I was until I got to college. I wrote a lot in high school—bless my high school teacher of English the last three years—but my writing consisted only of book reports, essay tests, note taking, and occasional research papers. During college at Miami University, though, I took four quarters of fiction writing taught by Milton White. I started paying attention to dramatically representing characters, writing with sensory detail and specificity, crafting words on the page. Later, as a young teacher, the territory of writing opened further when I read *Hooked on Books* (Fader and McNeil 1968). I began to keep a journal along with my students, became, in fact, obsessive about that daily, contemplative writing. The journal caused me to begin to respect all my writing, especially that which expressively poured out of me in barely legible, unedited handwriting. I described, recalled, complained, relived, speculated, praised, marveled, discovered, sometimes stuttering, but always working hard to be honest and direct. I tried out the skills and writing assignments I had my students do. And finally, at twenty-nine years old, after reading Marge Piercy's poetry on the recommendation of a former student, I wrote my first free verse poem—in my journal. Oh, yes, I'm for multiple genres. I'm for teachers pushing students into genre promiscuity.

For years my writing world was bereft. So many genres out there to explore and bend and express ourselves in, and so niggling had I been in what I wrote. I won't let similar narrowness guide my students who are now primarily college juniors preparing to teach English in secondary schools. I want them to carry my bias for genre inclusiveness into their own classrooms and affect countless teenagers. I want writers in high school, college, and beyond to contribute to the big world mural of writing, to experiment audaciously in many different genres, not ~~merely~~ only exposition.

7

Narrative Thinking

MULTIGENRE WRITING CALLS FOR STUDENTS TO USE NARRATIVE thinking (Elbow 1990, 191), thinking that renders experience, thinking that reveals rather than explains, thinking that shows more than it tells. It isn't that discursiveness, formal analysis, and exposition are bad. On the contrary, that kind of critical thinking is vital for all of us to develop. I do not, however, want a world in which people don't learn through and express themselves in narrative thinking, through images, figurative language, stories, and poetry. These forms have the capacity to reach readers' minds *and* emotions. Whitman (1855, 52) has a great quotation to think about:

> Logic and sermons never convince,
> The damp of the night drives deeper into my soul.

We could debate "never convince." There is plenty of logic and analysis out there that is both rationally convincing and emotionally moving—the summation of Atticus Finch in *To Kill a Mockingbird* (Lee 1960), for example, the personal essays of Anne Lamott (1999, 2005) and the memoir, *There If You Need Me*, by Kate Braestrup (2007). Still, I understand the spirit of Whitman's lines. Many teachers, in fact, have gone even farther than narrative thinking to get students to embrace other ways of knowing and communicating. They encourage and even require students to go beyond words altogether to include in their multigenre projects drawings, photographs, paintings, and other visual elements.

While expository forms like clear explanations, succinct position statements, and tight arguments surely have a place in multigenre papers, genres of narrative thinking carry the cognitive load. Such genres transport readers deeply into the subject matter, making the experience powerful, vivid, and pleasurable.

Carrie, an undergraduate, investigated artistic intelligence. She wondered if getting teenagers to employ artistic thinking might help them write better, even understand literature more deeply. Carrie wanted to know why some students continued to grow as artists and other students stopped making art altogether. This poem was part of her multigenre paper:

Grey Area

As a little girl, I studied my mom
while she wrote the weekly grocery list.
I mimicked her hand gestures,
the way her arm moved
back and forth, around,
then a dot here,
a slash somewhere up there,
then begin to flow once again.

When I was certain I had made the same gestures
using my hand-me-down Crayola Crayons,
I ran to my mom
eager for her to praise me
for learning to write at such a young age.

"No," she said, "those are not words,
but that is a beautiful picture.
Here, let me hang that on the fridge."

Carrie Stanek Ferrari, college junior

Carrie's poem requires heightened reading. I must visualize, examine characters' behavior, make inferences from their actions, make my own meanings. Her title is playful and deceptively simple. This poem is about intellect, the grey matter of the brain. But as this narrative poem plays out, I look back to the title and think of grey areas, too, those places that are not this or that, those places where it is difficult to discern a clear message. The matter at hand is ambiguous, complicated, grey. Mom values a certain kind of grey matter—verbological. Those are not words, she says. But she recognizes her daughter's achievement, judges it refrigerator worthy. Carrie's move to communicate in words does not meet Mom's criteria for writing. But the art is lovely and should be touted. In one view Mom is teaching Carrie distinctions between means of expression and communication. In another view, Mom devalues the child's art by ranking it second to words, even though she rewards Carrie's achievement.

Well, which interpretation is it then?

I say both.

Carrie gives readers room to think. Her poem is emphatically implicit. Emphatic implicitness is what artists strive for—to be clear and vivid and meaningful without being heavy-handed, without rhetorical jabs in the ribs. Being emphatically implicit means that writers apply the best they know about writing craft and trust readers to do their part. Emphatic implicitness is what Milton White wanted us fledging fiction writers to achieve.

In "Grey Area" Carrie renders experience. She doesn't explain. She doesn't analyze. She narrates an indelible moment through a free verse poem and expects readers to make meaning. I want students to have opportunities to write that way throughout their school experience, along with opportunities to explain, analyze, and persuade. Multigenre places students in a situation that demands narrative thinking. It's risky. Readers might not "get" the writer's intentions. Writers must work hard on the writing. They must craft it. That's what I want. Students grapple with the same dilemmas that poets, playwrights, and fiction writers do. That's multigenre.

TWENTY-FIVE YEARS SINCE THE MULTIGENRE IDEA PERCOLATED in me. I've written articles, chapters, and a book about multigenre. I've given keynote addresses and conducted workshops about multigenre. I've taught summer courses for teachers about multigenre. After seventeen years teaching high school students, in 1991, I began teaching college students at Utah State University. In an English department, my teaching schedule included courses in fiction writing, literature for teachers, and young adult literature. Winter quarter I supervised student teachers.

I didn't see how multigenre might fit into my teaching, didn't really give it a thought, so overwhelmed was I with the responsibility of college teaching, wondering if I was intellectually up to the work. One course I taught that first quarter was Advanced English Methods—a graduate course we offered one night a week fifty miles away at Salt Lake Community College. It was part of our master's degree in The Theory and Practice of Writing. I had ordered current and classic texts to read, planned units for expressive writing and poetry writing, and figured I'd spend one evening telling teachers about multigenre, sharing with them the work of my former high school students.

I talked about my plans for the course with a good friend I'd made at USU, Ken Brewer—poet and head of the graduate program in English. Ken knew about my multigenre work, had told me, in fact, that I was the only other person he'd ever met who had read *The Collected Works of Billy the Kid*. When I told him about my meager plans for multigenre, he frowned.

"What's wrong?" I asked.

"Make 'em write one," said Ken.

"What?"

"Make 'em write one. That's the way they'll understand multigenre."

Of course—make 'em write one.

That fall I got a sense of what graduate students were capable of creating when turned loose to write a research paper in multiple genres. Just as with high school students three years earlier, I was taken aback by how powerful, creative, intellectually responsible, and adventurous their work was. I've never looked back.

The *'em* of Ken's directive to "make 'em write one" was adults—undergraduates and graduate students who are often K–12 teachers. I've taught and learned with 'em since 1991. In the pages ahead I'll share what I've learned about teaching multigenre since I wrote *Blending Genre, Altering Style: Writing Multigenre Papers* (2000). Sometimes that learning has come because my pedagogical sensor has indicated I needed to make a task clearer or plug some gap in the assignment. Often, however, what I've learned is because a student has taken me intellectually and emotionally to a place I did not know I could go.

9

Multigenre
Before
Multigenre

MULTIGENRE WRITING HAS A LONG HISTORY: IN THE 1930S, John Dos Passos published a trilogy of novels titled *U.S.A.: The 42nd Parallel* (1930), *1919* (1932), and *The Big Money* (1936). The books are fiction and yet they are more than fiction, capturing at once the author's autobiographical experience and the sweep of America from 1900 to 1930, its culture, characters, history, and politics (Hart 1965, 233). In addition to narrative that reveals the lives of twelve fictional characters, Dos Passos breaks up those longer chapters with brief interchapters composed of experimental techniques he invents:

"The Newsreel," a collage of contemporary headlines, advertisements, lyrics from popular songs.

"The Camera Eye," impressionistic stream of consciousness sections from the author's autobiographical point of view.

"Thumbnail Biographies" of notable personages of the era, like Henry Ford, Thomas Edison, and the Unknown Soldier from World War I.

Intermixed with the prose fiction now and then are simple, line drawings depicting characters and plot moments.

To capture his picture of America both particular and national, Dos Passos avails himself of more than straight fictional prose. He uses poetry, stylized nonfiction, collage, montage, stream of consciousness, historically accurate accounts, drawings—multigenre.

Let's go back farther. In 1851 Herman Melville published *Moby Dick*. In 1969 Tom Romano read it. For decades I remembered it simply as a novel. When I examined it recently, though, I discovered more genre complexity than I remembered in that book published more than a century-and-a-half ago. After the table of contents (something you don't often find in a novel), readers encounter "Etymology," which explains the origin of *whale* and how it is spelled and pronounced in thirteen languages. Following this are twelve pages of quotations about whales from literature and the Bible, one quote after another with no words by a narrator linking them, providing context, or explaining what each has to do with the tale he will tell. All this genre variety readers take in before their eyes land upon "Call me Ishmael." Melville trusts readers to take in what he views as important information to the narrative ahead. And even in that narrative, Melville experiments, breaking the form of traditional fictional prose. Some chapter titles, for instance, are followed by parentheses containing what I think of as stage directions for scene and character. Chapter Forty appears like a modern musical with the name of a character (sailors from twenty different countries) followed by the lines he speaks or song lyrics he sings. In some instances Melville includes long footnotes in tiny print about some aspect of weather or animals. Melville, one of America's great writers from way-back-when, was, it must now be revealed, a multigenre experimenter!

I can go back even farther. Fifty years before *Moby Dick*, with "rare double genius," English painter-poet-engraver William Blake etched "his poems and drawings onto copper plates." The poems, in effect, were "cradled" within his illustrations. These he printed by hand, in color, to produce an "illuminated book" (Phillips 1997, 26).

Multigenre has a long history, longer, no doubt, than I realize. Our students can extend that practice, incorporating traditional genres, as well as employing other means of communication they have come to know in the twenty-first century.

I WANT TO SHOW YOU ONE COMPLETE MULTIGENRE PAPER before I move on to the specific ways I teach students to write them. I have many to choose from.

My students these last twenty-two years have been undergraduates, graduate students seeking teaching licensure, and teachers in graduate programs. They have written about a multitude of topics. They have researched and written about books they love—what I call a Lit-Based Multigenre paper that grew out of an NCTE presentation by Michelle Wood of Cedarville University in Ohio. Students have written about books as diverse as *The Phantom Toll Booth* by Norton Juster and *One Flew Over the Cuckoo's* Nest by Ken Kesey, *Nappy Hair* by Carolivia Herron and *The Awakening* by Kate Chopin, *The Secret Life of Bees* by Sue Monk Kidd and *Dracula* by Bram Stoker. Students have written about topics of personal interest: zombies, surrogate motherhood, eating locally, Japanese fox spirits, coffee shops, traveling abroad (written by a teacher who had taught in Europe fifteen years, a paper that prompted me to start leaving a tip on the pillow of my hotel room). Students have written out of the countryside of the soul, often involving family: the death of a fifteen-year-old son from leukemia, the search for a distant relative, child sexual abuse that rendered the author mute for two years, growing up as an undertaker's daughter, being an identical twin. I have yet to be bored with the topics students choose, even ones that don't spark my immediate interest, like the development of America's interstate highway system.

Most multigenre papers I've read these last twenty-two years have been tied to a specific assignment in my methods course. Each fall my students spend a month observing and teaching in public schools: two weeks in a middle school classroom, two weeks in a high school classroom—all morning, five days a week. For many, the shock is profound. For the first time, they experience school from the other side of the desk. For the first time, perhaps, they rise well before dawn to start the day. For the second of these field experiences—after they've read several multigenre papers—students write their own out of their experience as participant-observers and their growing moxie about education, teaching, and learning.

I give students a page of tips and strategies for writing their papers. My first tip is:

> Don't Plan: Not too much. And surely don't plan before you get into the context of your classroom and school. You might list genres to remind yourself of writing possibilities. But let the multigenre paper take shape from your experience teaching and learning in your particular classroom. Write extensively in your Field Notebook; you'll discover what interests you.

One of my students who had written a previous multigenre paper commented upon my advice:

> The curious thing about the writing process with multigenre is that it can be difficult to know where you're going until you're already there. Your first tip is "Don't Plan." I see why you say this. It's difficult to map out this paper. But "Don't Plan" doesn't mean "Don't Think." Multigenre takes time. Ideas and stories and themes need to marinate. In my experience, the marinating time is some of the most precious in writing a multigenre paper. My experiences and the notes I take about them are the ingredients of my brainstorming, prewriting, and revising. As I record and review my notes and reflect upon my observations, I am rooting myself in the multigenre writing process, a process that requires not stringent planning, but rather investment of time, patience, and heart.
>
> *Holly Jeric, college junior*

Several years ago, Sarah Halverson was one of those writers who invested time, patience, and heart. In addition to studying to be a teacher, Sarah minored in German and ice-skated competitively. Now a high school English teacher, Sarah was twenty years old when she wrote "Motivation Massacre 2007."

Figure 10–1 "Motivation Massacre"

*Witnessing the lack of motivation in one high school classroom.**

Sarah Halverson
Multigenre Paper
EDT 427
Dr. Romano
November 13, 2007

* All names of places and people are pseudonyms so as to maintain confidentiality.

(continued)

Obituaries: October 29, 2007
<u>Deceased:</u> <u>Motivation</u>
Cause of death: Lowered Expectations

Motivation was found early Monday morning barely breathing as he crawled around the corner of Stout St. trying to make it to Smith High School in time for the first bell. He was bleeding heavily from the side of the head but still valiantly carrying on in search of the students he was to meet with that day in school. When authorities found Motivation, 911 was immediately dialed but tragically it was too late to save him, and he died later that afternoon at the Good Hope Hospital.

An eye-witness observer later told investigative authorities that he saw Lowered Expectations side-swipe Motivation as she flew around the corner in her red corvet on her way in to school that morning. Motivation's brave attempts to continue on in his pursuit of students were just not enough to make up for his 60 mile-per-hour encounter with Lowered Expectations. We can only hope that Lowered learned her lesson: traveling at 60 mph may help you reach your destination faster, but faster is not always better when students' Motivation is at stake.

Where does a lack of movitvation begin?

Ms. L: Where did we leave off in the reading yesterday? We got through chapter 3 didn't we?

Me: Not in every class, I don't think.

Ms. L: Crap. I pulled a quiz for them to do today from online and it's over chapter 3. How much do they have left?

Me: Second block finished, but first block still has maybe 8 or so pages left to read.

Ms. L: Oh, great. They can finish that in like 15 minutes and then take 30 to take the quiz. I'm telling you, you can find so much stuff online; you don't have to do anything yourself.

> * Okay, wow. She didn't remember where we left off in the reading or which class read what, and she pulled a quiz from an online site and she couldn't even answer the questions on it herself because she hadn't read the book yet either. No wonder she has such low expectations of her students, she has such low expectations for herself. „You don't have to do anything yourself." But isn't that the point of teaching? Aren't we supposed to make sure we're creating the best activites for our studednts? If we don't have a passion for what we teach, how

(continued)

are we supposed to motivate our students to love English—
reading, writing, poetry, alliteration, the beauty of the written
and spoken word! This is indeed going to be a very interesting
experience. This morning makes me wonder—why this total lack
of motivation? *

(Sign posted on the wall of Ms.L's classroom.)

> **"I am convinced that life is 10% what happens to me and 90% how I react."**

Smith High School

Visitor Pass

Name Motivated to Raise Expectations
Date Each day for 2 weeks
Time to change

Believing Labels: Motivating Low Expectations
(Dialogue from instruction in Ms.L's English II class)

Me: Okay, on this activity I want to you choose your scene from the novel and
explain to me why it is important to you as well as why it is important to the rest of
the novel.

Darnell: WHAT?! Maybe you haven't heard this Ms. H, but we're a remedial
class… we don't write answers like that.

Mike: Yeah! Just tell us what the right answer is!

Halverson 3

Me: The answer is your own. You need to come up with your own idedas about why you chose your scene and then choose information from the novel to support your ideas; as long as you support your answer, you can't be wrong.

Darnell: (disappointedly) Man, we don't do this.

```
LABEL: remedial learner
CAUTION: not intelligent
```

(Another dialogue from second block)

Me: (handing Nate a worksheet on idioms) Here Nate—try to have it completed by the end of the period.

Nate: Man, Ms. H, there's too much writing on this page! I ain't doin' this!

Me: Yes, you are. You are perfectly capable of doing this worksheet.

Nate: No I'm not! I'm on an IEP! You have to accommodate!

```
LABEL: IEP kid
CAUTION: not capable
```

Obituaries: November 2, 2007
Deceased: Motivation
Cause of death: Family Environment

Motivation was found in the basement of a small ranch house on Paternal Lane last Friday evening curled into a corner; authorities estimate his last breath had left him just hours before. From the autopsy report, it was clear that ~~Mitovation~~ Motivation had suffered a long, drawn out and painful death from starvation and neglect.

Motivation was born a strong, sturdy lad that always tried his very best at everything he put his mind to—walking, talking, pointing out all the correct words to go with the pictures his kindergrarten teacher showed him—but his health was constantly tried by Family Environment. Family Environment used to taunt him, "Why are you trying so hard? You need not try; I never did, and you'll be just like me in the end—you are, after all, my own."

~~Eventually,~~ over the years, Motivation grew weak and stopped trying at all. He spent most of his time in front of the television with Opportunity; the two of them sat together, killing braincells one by one and slowly wasting away to nothing. Motivation took to the basement only days before his untimely death when Family Environment began to ~~simply~~ ignore Motivation's very existence. As the paramedics removed Motivation's body early on Saturday morning, Family Environment looked on in disbelief, "I did that?" She asked, and her voice was barely above a whisper as the ambulence pulled away, carrying Motivation with it.

(continued)

SMITH HIGH SCHOOL REPORT CARD: QUARTER 1

Name: Deacon, Darnell J.   Student ID: 1867320-B
Grade: Sophomore   Home Room: 256

Subject:	Letter Grade:	Comments:
English II	D+	29, 36
Remedial Math	F	36
Earth Science	D	29, 42
Health	C	36, 42
Government	F	29

Tardy: 15 days   Absent: 4 days

Comment Codes:
29: Unmotivated in class
36: Missing and late assignments
42: Lack of class participation

**Parent
Signature
Required.**

X: *Don't Bother me With this*

X: *Face Yourown Consequences*

As I enter the room my first Tuesday morning:
Ms. L: Your life got a little easier as of yesterday.

Me: (completely confused) Why is that?

Ms. L: Two of my second block Monday/Wednesday boys just got suspended for 10 days. They got into a fight right after you left while they were working on their papers on the computers in my classroom.

Me: Wow, seriously?! What was the fight about?

Halverson 5

Ms. L: Kel was making fun of Kevin because of all those designs he has cut into his hair—he said they looked ridiculous that that Kevin was „trippin` when he had them done.

Me: And that started a fight? Like, a fist-fight? All out?

Ms. L: Yep. That's all it takes with these kids. They have no parental involvement and no consequences at home. Kevin actually got out his cell phone and called his mom to ask if she would be mad if he „beat the crap out of this kid."

Me: What did she tell him?

Ms. L: She told him he could decide on his own and take the consequences; she didn't care. So, he went at Kel and they had to be physically separated and then written up and suspended. But don't worry, you didn't want them here anyway.

> * I didn't want them here anyway? Actually, I talked with Kevin for a few minutes yesterday... I think I did want him here. Don't we want them all here? I would hope so, whether it makes my life a little more difficult or not. I can't believe his mom actually told him she didn't care what he did—what kind of parent says that to her son? *

Field Notes: It's oddly quiet in here today. We just finished chapter four in *Of Mice and Men* and they are taking a quiz over it right now. This class is rarely ever quiet, even when they are supposed to be, so it is really strange in here right now. I feel like the quiet in the room is almost palpable—it's so awkward and out of place—like that elephant in the corner that everyone sees but no one really acknowledges is there. Or maybe it's just me. Nate just walked into the room 40 minutes late for first block with no excused tardy note. Ms. L says he has a history of coming to school high; she just looked over in his direction and told me, „Oh, he's stoned out of his mind. He's completely and totally out of it." Her assuredness makes me wonder if he is really high...

(15 minutes pass)

I just finished trying to help Nate with his vocabulary activity. I think Ms. L is probably right, unfortunately enough. He didn't understand things that he normally wouldn't have needed clarification on, and more than that, nothing he said made any sense! He even had trouble staying upright in his seat without losing his balance. How does this happen? I can't even begin to

(continued)

Halverson 6

comprehend this! I asked Ms. L how he has the means to come to school high and she said she knows his family history and his mom doesn't care. She just pretends it isn't happening if she sees it, but she's rarely home when he is anyway. He has no one holding him accountable for his actions; if it feels good at the moment, he does it. Wow. That degree of parental ambivalence is absolutely beyond my comprehension. What should we do? I feel like just leaving him in class, high, while all the other students inform him ever so loudly that he's trippin' can't be the best solution. But then again, at least he's here, right?

RINGRING***RING***
Mom: Hello! How ya doin' Rory?
(I can hear her smile through her voice in my ear and that in turn makes me smile too.)
Me: Why hello Lorelei, I'm doing okay, just tired is all. The students are really great, and they're absolutely hilarious, but they're just not motivated to do any work, or to try to succeed.
Mom: That would be pretty frustrating to work with… how are they with you? Do they listen?
Me: Mostly they do. Well, not today though…first block was a mess. They chewed me up and spit me out! I had to split up these two kids because they absolutely WOULD NOT stop talking! But really I called for a different reason.
Mom: Really, what's that?
Me: Thanks mom.
Mom: For what? (she laughs)
Me: For being my mom. Really being there, no matter what. For expecting my best and always believing in my dreams.
Mom: Aww, sweetie, of course I did! I love you. But what brought on this sudden thank you?
Me: A lot of the kids have parents that just don't care. It's so hard for them to be motivated to do well when their parents expect nothing of them and half of them don't even know or care what's going on in their kid's life. Just, thank you mom. For being so amazing.

Mom: (I can hear her smile again as she speaks…) Nothing less would do.

(continued)

Obituaries: November 6, 2007
<u>**Deceased**</u>: <u>**Motivation**</u>
Cause of death: Social Pressure

Motivation was rushed by care flight to Good Hope Hospital Monday morning after he was attacked at school by a group of teenagers in search of some trouble. Motivation was sitting in the library using one of the school's computers to finish a paper for Ms.L's English class when Social Pressure came to find him. He asked Motivation to go on a walk with him behind gym on the back lawn. Motivation noticed that Social Pressure had brought his lackies with him, so he consented to go.

Once they were on the back lawn, out of sight of any administrators, Social Pressure began to get to Motivation. "Why are you always doing what the teacher asks you to do? Why do you turn in your work on time? Why are you so eager to participate in class—what do you think, you're going to college?" Motivation lost the will to try to stammer out the answers when Social Pressure and his lackies began to close in on him. They punched, jabbed, kicked, and scratched every inch of Motivation they could get to. By the time a teacher at the school intervened, Motivation was barely recognizable. By the time the care flight arrived at the hospital, it was too late—Motivation had slipped into a deep coma from which he would never awake.

George on Social Isolation: "I ain't got no people. I seen the guys that go around on the ranches alone. That ain't no good. They don't have no fun."
~John Steinbeck

"The deck is stacked...against you."
(In the hall during class change)
Ms. L: You better get going mark, you're going to be late again and you know you already have too many tardies this quarter.
Mark: You just say that because you' racist.
Dustin (Mark's friend): Yeah Ms. L, you' racist!
Ms. L: I think we all know that's a ridiculous accusation.
Danielle: (from down the hall) Ms. L's not racist! You' just upset because you' late again.
Mark: You're such a teacher's pet, I bet you write essays for fun.
Danielle: I'm not even gonna bother with you anymore.
Ms. L: (to me) They all back each other up, like what happened with Dustin and Mark, once you lose one of them the rest just follow one by one...
Me: Why is that?
Ms. L: They stick together, and for some of these kids doing work and respecting teachers is a one-way ticket to having no one to hang out with after school.

Damien on Social Groups: "You gotta hang with your boys, you know? That's where it's at."   ~Sophomore, English II student at Smith High

(continued)

Field Notes: *I got asked today if I was racist. I told Nate I wasn't and he seemed to take my answer for the truth, which was refreshing. Sometimes they just seem to want to disagree with the teachers just for the heck of it. They all band together against school work. They have so much potential! I just don't know yet how to unlock it. One decides that wanting academic success isn't cool and the rest seem to slowly follow suit until they are all doing work that is below what they are really capable of—that combined with the expectations being set so low by teachers to begin with makes it so difficult for these kids to stay motivated to succeed. It makes me sad. It makes me angry! I want to do something about it, but in just 2 weeks how much can I really do here? I know one thing though: I'm going to try. I'm going to expect these kids to connect to this book personally even if they try to kill me in the process. In fact, I bet if I explain all this stuff in the right way, they'll even like the change. Yeah, that's it. . .that's the solution, at least for now. They may not be motivated, but I am! They're smart and I know they can show it.*

Obituaries: November 8, 2007
<u>Deceased</u>: <u>Motivation</u>

Cause of death: Lowered Expectations, Family Environment, and Social Pressure

Motivation's body has yet to be found in the days since his disappearance and apparent murder. It was common knowledge that Lowered Expectations and Social Pressure were sworn enemies of Motivation, so authorities questioned them first when Motivation suspiciously went missing. The two of them denied responsibility but the investigator was not satisfied with their story that Motivation simply ran away. The Private Eye then decided to question Family Environment since she and Motivation spent so much time together. At first, she corroborated Social Pressure's story that Motivation had picked up and walked out, leaving no forwarding address, but after several hours of intense questioning she cracked.

After Family Environment's confession the police took her and her accomplices (Lowered Expectations and Social Pressure) into custody for collaborative homicide. Though none of the three would tell investigators where they hid the body, it became evident after the interviews that Motivation was tied up and thoroughly beaten before being left in an undisclosed location to slowly die. The three face life in prison without parole. A memorial service will be held for Motivation on Saturday, November 10, 2007 at the Church in the Park on Determination Drive. He will be sorely missed.

(continued)

(continued)

Dialogue with a Student during instruction:

Me: Hey Ben, you need to stop talking and focus on your work... you have a good image there, now tell me why it's important to the novel.

Ben: Because we learn Lennie gets in trouble but George protects him; it's foreshadowing Lennie's problems at the Ranch.

Me: Great! Now why is it important to you?

Ben: Man, I get in trouble all the time, but my friends always got my back. Kinda like Lennie and George.

Me: That's awesome Ben! You've got it, now just write it down on your paper.

Ben: Yeah, it's awesome! Man, Ms. H, I'm smart!

Me: I believe it!

Editorials: November 9, 2007

A letter for those close to Motivation in their time of mourning:

Dear Friends,

The loss of Motivation in our schools and daily lives is indeed a tragedy. We lift him up at this time, and all those especially close to him; he was a remarkable human being who did not deserve the harsh treatment he received from those around him. This time is trying but those of us who believed in Motivation and all he had to offer must not lose hope! Remember that Motivation is survived by his four siblings: Initiative, Inspiration, Drive, and Desire. We must nourish their growth and help them develop and make their presence known in our schools and communities. Take heart friends, all is not lost.

Sincerely,

Silver Lining

Halverson 11

Motivation Massacre 2007 Note Page:

1. Each time there is a change in subject there is an obituary for the concept of motivation, which has been personified and then murdered by one of three other characters (Lowered Expectations, Family Environment, and Social Pressure). I chose this format for my repetend because the thing that stuck out to me more than anything else as I interacted with the students at the high school I went to was their lack of motivation. These obituaries are very important to the overall paper and to me because it was so disheartening to see such a lack of desire and drive in these students—motivation really was dead for the majority of students at that school. My heart broke for them.

2. Dialogue occurs frequently in this paper due to the nature of the conversations I had with the teacher and the students. They were dynamic, important conversations and needed to be used in the paper to show the reality of each of these "murderers'" attacks on student motivation. There is at least one dialogue between me and the teacher or students in each section and two of the dialogues are followed by indented sections surrounded with asterisks; these sections are the thoughts that went through my mind after the exchange was over. They are kind of like my own little journal entry related to the conversation in that they are my own, candid, real thoughts associated with what I just heard.

3. I think it is important to note a few things about the telephone conversation with my mom on page 6. My mom really did answer the phone and ask „How ya doing Rory?" My mom and I use nick names taken from the Television show Gilmore Girls and jokingly refer to each other in that way sometimes. Rory is Lorelei's daughter and the two are very close— best friends as well as mother and daughter. I chose to include these names in my paper because it emphasizes the close relationship I have with my mom and how much I appreciate her; this point was particularly important because it is situated within a section of my paper that discusses the students' lack of parental support. This appreciation for my mom and dad and everything they did for me was something that I felt very strongly after hearing of some of the students' family problems. My mom knows how much I appreciate and love her, but I wanted to call to thank her again because this field make me realize anew how much my family's constant support had touched every area of my life and motivated me to succeed and believe in myself.

4. The four square reading quiz as well as the references to the Of Mice and Men lesson in the sections about are all references to a quiz that I took from Carol Jago and then modified so it would work well with the students I was working with. In the first square they described a scene from the novel that was important to them in one sentence, the second square was a drawing of the scene, the third square was an explanation of why it was important to them and to the novel as a whole, and the fourth square was for a quote they found from the book to support their image as being important. (I chose to include an image as each square in my quiz for this paper rather than adopt the exact same format as the quiz I gave the students.) This comprehension acitivity required them to think for themselves and decide what was important to them; they were perfectly capable of completing it if they would take that step beyond being told the answers and out of their comfort zone. I hoped it would give them the encouragement they needed to want to excel, and for some of them I think it truly helped.

(continued)

Halverson 12

Works Cited

Steinbeck, John. *Of Mice and Men.* New York, New York: Penguin Books USA Inc.,

1937.

II

Assignment and Preparation

Before I plant my garden, I prepare. In November I till fallen leaves into the soil. In January I order seeds and supplies. In April I till in nutrients and begin to plan the architecture of my planting. I approach teaching multigenre the same way. I show students how to search for ideas, develop topics, begin research. When they begin writing, I want the bed of creativity prepared.

11

The Many Ways of Multigenre

MY FIRST FORAY INTO THE ASSIGNMENT REQUIRED STUDENTS to write about a person of fame or infamy—their choice. This is still, I believe, a rewarding way to write multigenre; compelling personal interest and dynamic human drama drives students. In my classes now, however, and in the classes of other teachers, multigenre has encompassed more.

I require students to incorporate research into multigenre papers, regardless of their subject, even if they write from deeply personal experience. In "Living with Death: Growing Up as an Undertaker's Daughter," Jessica wrote an engaging multigenre paper revealing how her family was affected by her father's profession. Through inquiry she deepened her understanding by researching death and dying, casket technology, and methods of embalming and cremation. She read books, articles, websites, watched a film, and interviewed family members. Amid her research revelations, she wove stories, grim realities, and occasional humor that she knew as an insider.

What are your passions, your driving interests, your consuming issues: Vampires? The development of the interstate highway system in the 1950s? The 1994 genocide in Rwanda? Punk rock? The film version of *The Wizard of Oz*? The California Gold Rush? The mill girls of Lowell, Massachusetts? America's perfect novel? The 2001 race riots in Cincinnati? The egg? (A delightful, skillfully written, serious and whimsical look at the egg throughout history, biology, evolution, and culture.)

Or maybe your topic represents a strong intersection of experience and research: Alzheimer's disease and the decline of your grandfather, the United States Marine Corp and your fervent desire to enter the Marines after NROTC training, your desire to become a teacher and the legacy of a renowned educator, your belief in social justice and your passion for Richard Wright's *Native Son*, special education and the first-hand knowledge you have of your younger brother's struggle with a learning disability.

I don't believe there is an iteration of the multigenre paper that would surprise me. Remember Whitman: "I am large, I contain multitudes." Teachers have shaped multigenre to their curriculum, as I have done in having students write them out of their field experiences in schools. One teacher has students write multigenre papers about their favorite authors, even emulating the author's style and voice. My daughter, a high school English teacher, has her students explore the "common elements and tensions" between *Their Eyes Were Watching God* and *The Awakening*. Students in history classes have written multigenre papers about an historical event or movement. Education majors in a capstone course abroad that compared European schools with those in the United States have written multigenre papers that blended experience, culture, and research. My science education colleague at Miami has students write multigenre projects about a life science organism.

Regardless of their topic choice, I provide guidance to support students along their creative, intellectual, multigenre journey. Below is my combination assignment/pep talk/cautionary advice that I give to undergraduates enrolled in a writing course I teach called Crafting a Written Voice:

Multigenre Research Paper EDT 180B

Multigenre Research Papers

This is a chance to pursue a passion in your intellectual/emotional/spiritual life, a chance to strive to answer a question involving a topic of consuming interest to you and to communicate your learning through a multigenre research project, where you get at the factual, the emotional, and the imaginative. This is a time to be expansive, to try the untried.

Choose a person, idea, topic, trend, era, cultural phenomenon, movement, thing, place . . . and become the quintessential, wigged-out mad researcher on the trail of information vital to achieving peace of mind and satisfying your insatiable curiosity.

Required Research Sources of Your Inquiry:
- At least one book (or two, or three. Read fast, annotate, become an expert)
- Articles

- Primary material: interviews, testimony, observations, surveys
- Internet sources[1]

Genres/Pieces/Elements Your Multigenre Project Must Contain:
- Brief expository piece, 250–350 words. Make this vivid, informational, straight-ahead writing or craft a tight, driving argument. Boil down your topic to essentials. This piece can appear as a straight mini-essay, or you can drop the exposition into a form that fits your multigenre paper.
- Preface/Introduction/Dear Reader
- Poetry in contemporary free verse style
- Prose Poem
- Flash Fiction/Nonfiction
- A visual element
- Bibliography
- Endnotes
- Unifying elements (golden thread, repetend, repeated images, genres answered, fragmented narrative, a detail mentioned in one brief piece exploded and illustrated in a longer piece deeper in the paper)

You must include all nine bulleted items in your paper. You'll need to write more genres than the ones I've listed, however, to create a fully realized multigenre experience. Whatever else you write is up to you. Range widely as you create this paper. Your intellect and sensibility are capable of inventiveness and surprising connections. Go for this.

One tip: begin your research soon, make it part of your academic life, take notes, and capture bibliographic information as you read, which

---

[1] The Internet is democratic. You know it holds surprising, helpful information. And since there is no screening on the Internet, you'll also encounter misinformation, balderdash, and lies. Be careful. Learn who sponsors a website and what its purpose and bias are. Gauge the quality and the depth of what you find in cyberspace. I definitely don't want you to simply paste material from a website into your paper. I want to see an original multigenre paper from you, one passionate and grounded in a thorough research understanding of your topic. I want to see you expand your knowledge about some subject, maybe even develop wisdom. I want to see you stretch and refine your writing skills and powers of communication. I want you to use the thinking we've done about writing with a distinctive voice. I want to read your paper and be informed, but even more, I want to be *moved*.

will save you time and tedium later. Immerse yourselves so the writing comes easy. Such immersion will lead to surprises, connections, ideas, and—dare I say—creativity.

The bulleted requirements give students something to check their progress against, something to write in and around. Some of the bullets—the preface/introduction/dear reader, bibliography, endnotes, and unifying elements—will help students write quality multigenre papers. Other bullets—prose poem, flash fiction, free verse poetry, visual element, and exposition—will push students to try genres they might not write on their own (in Section III, I'll write more about genre possibilities).

I Can Do Something You Probably Cannot . . . Yet

After we have read the assignment and discussed preliminary questions, I pull out an old Samsonite briefcase jammed with thirty-five to forty multigenre papers on a wide range of topics. Each student chooses a couple and begins reading, dipping into the passions of past students who became immersed and genre free. The papers are all similar in that they are multigenre, but they are oh-so-different. Students take note of what earlier writers did that worked; they also see that there is no one way to write a multigenre paper.

Multigenre Anxiety

Don't be surprised to see multigenre anxiety set in, especially from students who have successful histories writing academic papers they've come to see as formulaic. Here is what I mean:

After reading my assignment and several field experience multigenre papers by past students, one young woman wrote a one-pager she titled "Multi-Genre Scared." Below is an excerpt:

A multigenre project makes me scared to even attempt it. I'm so used to getting good grades and doing well that the thought of not writing something great scares me. . . . I'm more intimidated than put at ease! I can't write like that! I can't compose something that doesn't have a specific form or guidelines to follow! I need structure! I need direction! I need spe-cifics! This is too much stress!

Katherine Lunt, college junior

Another wrote,

I could feel the anxiety creeping up inside me like a spider sneaking up my arm. How am I *ever* going to write like this? The thought both thrilled me and frightened me; on my left shoulder sat my traditional one point of view essay, and on my right sat my future multigenre paper.

Jaclyn Kamman, college junior

One tip I gave students before they went into their field experiences was not to plan their multigenre papers. I urged them to let the papers emerge from their observations of the classroom culture they would discover, the dynamic characters they would encounter, the issues and dramas that would come to dominate their thinking. My advice threw Kelsey into panic mode:

No planning?! Are you serious? I'm addicted to planning. I don't even start writing these one-pagers without a clear-cut outline to start with. Planning will be my downfall. I'm going to over think everything and hope it fits seamlessly into my paper. There are so many genres and so much free-dom in multigenre that I'm starting to worry. I don't like freedom. I like strict guidelines. I'm not one to flourish outside the box. How do I know if I'm being creative enough? What if I'm being too creative? AHHHHHH! *deep breath* No, just stop. I'm going to let things happen around me and I'm going to breathe them in. Then, I'm going to exhale them out through my writing. Whatever spills out is mine, and I will embrace it.

Kelsey Fallon, college junior

In the lead of her one-pager, Tori pinpointed the origins of her anx-iety: "Multigenres are madness and mayhem because they break every kind of mold student writers were ever forcefully fit and rigidly shaped in." She had written a multigenre paper two years earlier, as a first-year college student, and she had struggled:

Creativity is a scary thing. I never had the chance to write in creative styles in high school, as it took a back seat to what we were told was more formal and experienced writing. Creative writing and creative formatting and style are intimidating because there are no limits. Yes, there is a rubric. Yes, there are certain requirements, but there are a lot of gray areas as well. I wish I was confident enough to see the gray areas as an invitation for fun, for exploration, for learning, but lately I have been seeing them as a black hole—something I can't get too close to or I will be sucked in for the rest of time.

Tori Tarvin, college junior

"Sucked in for the rest of time"? By a multigenre project? Spiraling through space, riding multiple genres, leaping conventional boundaries, and, given the relativity of time, ol' Einstein out there just ahead of you? What a way to go!

Katherine, Jaclyn, Kelsey, and Tori all met the challenge of writing interesting, varied, substantive multigenre papers. Maybe the anxiety was useful in driving them forward. They wrote something that made you want to read. They revealed truths about their experience trying out their teaching chops with real teenagers in English language arts classrooms. In the end, they embraced multigenre. The intimidation of newness, the anxiety of not comprehending immediately what was expected, the daunting reality of so much unfamiliar work ahead, all these gave way to the pleasure of being sucked into a place of intellect, accomplishment, and creativity. Katherine gets the last word:

I am intimidated and scared to write this multigenre paper, but deep down I am excited. I am anxious to see what I come up with. Maybe I'll surprise myself and think of something out of the box and eye-catching. Maybe I'll write my best paper ever! I have to at least try. I owe it to myself to at least try. And by God, I AM going to try! Bring it on, multigenre paper! I will take you down!

Katherine Lunt, college junior

IN ADDITION TO HAVING STUDENTS READ ACTUAL PAPERS, I demonstrate multigenre through a segment from Ken Burns' *Jazz* (2001a). Burns is the greatest documentary filmmaker of our time. His award winning films include *The Civil War* (1990), *Baseball* (1994), *Not for Ourselves Alone: Elizabeth Cady Stanton and Susan B. Anthony* (1999), and *Unforgiveable Blackness: The Rise and Fall of Jack Johnson* (2004). His epic series, *Jazz* (18.5 hours), chronicles the development of this quintessential American music from its inception on slave plantations up through the twentieth century. Jazz is, Burns writes, "the only art form created by Americans, an enduring and indelible expression of our genius and promise" (Burns 2001b).

Burns is an artist whose new work I eagerly await. When *Jazz* aired on PBS in January 2001, I spent a couple hours most evenings over a two-week span watching the story of jazz. I say *story*, for that is what Burns is: a storyteller. You get caught up in the lives of characters, the twists and turns of plot, the intrigues, the triumphs, the luck, the terrible wrongs. As with any communicator, Burns has a point of view that has been shaped out of his inquiry and cultural experience. He has bias and points to prove. To do that, he draws you into story, which makes his explanations, character sketches, facts, and analyses entertaining, surprising, and, often, compelling.

The segment of *Jazz* that stands as the most perfect eighteen minutes of film making I've ever seen is "Mr. Armstrong," found in Episode 4: "The True Welcome." Born in 1901, Louis Armstrong played his trumpet in seven decades of American music. Burns notes that "the biggest surprise and delight of" his inquiry into jazz was "getting to know the power and force and genius of Louis Armstrong" (Burns 2001b). So much was I surprised and entertained by "Mr. Armstrong" that I watched it repeatedly, coming to know—as Burns had—Armstrong's power and genius beyond the gravelly voice and white handkerchief he flourished. Writes Burns,

Louis Armstrong is quite simply the most important person in American music. He is to 20th century music (I did not say jazz) what Einstein is to physics, Freud is to medicine and the Wright Brothers are to travel. He transformed first instrumental playing, liberating jazz, cutting it loose from nearly all constraints, essentially inventing what we call swinging, and then brought an equally great revolution to singing. (Burns 2001b)

As a teacher in America, I want Louis Armstrong's musical legacy to remain alive in the American consciousness. His contribution to music is a part of our past I want to conserve, just as I want to conserve the memory of Abraham Lincoln in politics, Elizabeth Cady Stanton in women's suffrage, Jack Dempsey in sport, Malcolm X in the ongoing quest for racial justice, and Crazy Horse for integrity, courage, and self-understanding. After viewing and discussing "Mr. Armstrong," my students' vague notions of the musician fade and are replaced by vivid images and stirring information Burns has researched and delivered with filmic artistry.

But what's the multigenre connection? It's this: Burns' film is documentary, but that term doesn't begin to capture the rich blend of genres and subgenres Burns has gathered and uses to communicate:

- Still photos (publicity shots, candid shots, portraits).
- Camera movement—more strategy than genre—as Burns pans over and slowly zooms in and out on the still photos.
- Live footage—an early sound film—of Armstrong and his band performing "Dinah, Dinah" to an audience of white patrons.
- Archival documentary film footage of New York City in the 1930s—its streets, landmarks, Harlem, people on the street, audiences applauding.
- Natural sounds of traffic, car horns, and applause dubbed into the silent, archival film footage.
- Talking heads: excerpts from eight different interviews with musicians, a critic, a biographer, a singer, and a ballplayer from the Negro baseball league. The comments from them are so deftly woven into the texture of the film that it doesn't seem there could have been eight of them.

- A clear, crafted script, blending narrative, exposition, and smooth transitional language to move from one segment to the next.
- The very voice of the narrator, distinctive, resonant, trusted.
- Excerpts from a *New York Sun* review of an Armstrong performance.
- A direct quote from Armstrong.
- Louis Armstrong's music, sometimes as background, sometimes as performance, sometimes as the point of analysis.
- A film within the film: a three-minute music video montage set to Armstrong singing "Black and Blue," bringing into focus America's legacy of racism.
- A quote from Charles L. Black, former professor of constitutional law at Yale, who saw Louis Armstrong perform and wrote years later, "He was the first genius I'd ever seen. It is impossible to overstate the significance of a sixteen-year-old southern boy seeing genius for the first time in a black person."

Get hold of *Jazz*. Watch episode four, "The True Welcome." You are a learner. You'll quicken to the multiple genres Burns employs to make vivid an era and an irreplaceable figure in twentieth-century American culture. "Mr. Armstrong" could turn out to be the best use of film you'll ever employ in the classroom.

13

Tilling the Garden

Idea Exploration and Research Design

CONFESSION: FOR YEARS AS A YOUNG TEACHER I MADE assignments to high school students but didn't help them find topics to write about. I'd give them a day in class to draft their writing, telling them beforehand when that day would be. We'd looked at samples of the kind of writing I wanted them to create and talked about its features, but I'd lead students into no idea generation strategies, no memory retrieval, no identification of their passions.

This is how I had been taught, by teachers who didn't write, but also by teachers in college who did write and should have known better. Both kinds of teachers expected you to complete writing assignments, but where an idea came from, how indelible images within us might lead to rich subject matter, how at first blush an idea might appear unpromising, and how—with nurturing—it might develop and grow rich in meaning and complexity . . . no one had talked about that. I believe this neglect of idea generation was part of an elitist culture of writing. IQ was all. If you were smart, ideas just came. You either had it or you didn't. Producing writing was a Hemingwayesque, macho game of independent critical thinking.

Writers didn't talk about ideas they might write about. They didn't talk about what they were writing. They wrote. They wrote complex novels that few understood. They wrote enigmatic short stories. They wrote poems that required footnotes for clarity. And they certainly weren't sentimental. Never did a teacher lead us in an activity that brought our passions to the fore, that moved us to see our specific experiences and interests as worthy material, that led us to list what we wanted to know more about, to make conscious what was unconscious but mattered deeply. We didn't talk in class about such grubby matters as searching out ideas. Gosh, I'm ashamed I perpetuated that elitist notion of writing. But there it is. It's part of where I'm from as a writing teacher. I must own it and move on.

Now, I pointedly give students time in class to cover the territory of their thinking, their values, their passions, their interests. After students have read several multigenre papers and we've talked about my assignment sheet, I give them time to dig around, turn over the soil of their interests, speculate about their "I wonders":

> "I love how an egg comes in its own package. I wonder what the egg has been like through history?"

> "We drove 250 miles yesterday in less than four hours. I wonder when the interstate highway system was built and whose idea it was?"

> "I watched a TV show about Jack the Ripper. I wonder why Scotland Yard couldn't catch him?"

I ask students to list their interests, their passions both big and little. I list mine at the moment: growing different varieties of tomatoes, Walt Whitman, writing, teaching writing, oral interpretation, buying/ leasing a car, swimming, Woody Guthrie and the 1930s, creative non-fiction, Pilot G-2 10 gel pens, the UNH mug I use each morn to drink strong black coffee made from House Blend beans bought at Kofenya, a coffee shop two college seniors started in uptown Oxford.

After students have spent time scouring around and talking about ideas as a big group, I assign them an idea exploration. They must bring to class, typed, five ideas they might pursue in a multigenre project, explaining why these ideas interest them. I let students talk in small groups about their papers. I know how such causal talk can lead to new topics and expansions of incipient ideas. I ask students to send me their papers electronically prior to class, so I can read them, comment, and return the document before we meet again. Note that I ask for five ideas, not one. Even though students might know immediately what they want to write about, I want them to maintain an attitude of exploration. I want to keep ideas in play, the door of topic choice open.

Below is a sample five-idea assignment from Chelsea Donovan, a college junior:

Five Multigenre Ideas with Annotations

1. **Eating Disorders.** Not just the clinical stuff, but what goes into the mindset of an eating disorder. How does it affect the people that surround that person? How does it go unnoticed?

   www.something-fishy.org/ is a pro recovery website that covers all types of eating disorders from anorexia to compulsive overeating. It also covers topics such as cultural factors and a section for helping loved ones. Also sites that are pro-ana will be looked at to get an inside view on what some people who suffer from eating disorders are thinking and doing.

   > All these topics are fertile territory, Chelsea. I'm glad you are making the decision to pick one, not me.

   > Some of the most powerful mg papers I've read over the last twenty years have been about this topic. They were especially powerful when the writer took us inside.

   > This is new to me. What is "pro-ana"?

2. **Sleeping.** What are the benefits of sleeping? How do people use sleeping? Naps- good or bad? Why do we get sleepy? Why do some people need more sleep than others? Why do you sleep more when you are depressed? Why do some people dream and others don't? www.sleepfoundation.org/article/sleep-topics/depression-and-sleep

   > This might seem mundane, but I think we have an inherent interest in this topic. You could teach readers all kinds of things.

3. **Ode to the Middle Child.** I've always wanted to write a letter or something to my little brother, the middle child in our family, thanking him for being who he is. I think there is something so special about middle children that should be celebrated. I think that they see the world differently from their place in the middle of the family. They have a different set of pressures being crammed in the middle of two other children, and I think that the sense of humor that comes out of it is unparalleled.

   www.time.com/time/health/article/0,8599,1672715,00.html

   > There is a lot of research you can access about children in the middle.

4. **Life with a high functioning, autistic mind.** I have always wondered what is going on in my little sister, Alison's, mind. She

has high functioning Autism, and she sees the world through a very different lens than I do. I can't tell you how many times I have thought that if I could only know how she thought then I could have a better idea of who she was and how to reach her. Through research about Autism and through talking to my sister and drawing from our life experiences together hopefully I can try to capture some of the inner workings of her mind.

Gosh, if you could capture this!

You would have the great advantage here of measuring what you learn through research with what you have lived with Alison. I'll bet this work would also illuminate experiences with Alison that you didn't understand or were frustrated by.

5. **Crying.** Where do tears come from? Why do some people cry all the time and other people hardly cry at all? Why do we cry when we are happy, or angry, or sad? What do tears do for us? How does it make us feel to see other people cry?

Another seemingly mundane topic that we all have interest in. Tears spring to my eyes easily. I'm a sucker for being overwhelmed by music or scenes in a movie, by moments in novels too.

Chelsea is on her way to finding a topic that matters, one that is inward, tied to her experience as sister, observer, survivor.

Research Design

The following week—after much talk, feedback, and further mulling—I require students to write research designs that ease them into their inquiry, asking them to take tentative first steps and initial exploration. The books of three friends led me to this requirement. In *The Multigenre Research Paper* (2001), Camille Allen describes how fifth-grade teacher Laurie Swistak has her students complete K-W-L charts about their topics before they begin researching.

K: What writers already know about their topic.

W: What writers want to know about their topic.

L: What writers learned about their topics after researching.

About the same time I read Allen's book, I was rereading *The Art of Classroom Inquiry* (1993) by Ruth Shagoury Hubbard and Brenda Miller Power. In that excellent book the authors describe how teachers write research designs before they begin qualitative inquiry in their classrooms, "a plan that calls for both discipline and imagination" (1993, 50). My research design for the multigenre paper is an amalgam of Allen and Hubbard/Miller with a bit of Romano thrown in. Students' initial foray into their inquiry is good for them as writers and me as teacher. Both of us become invested. And creating a research design thwarts that blackguard, Procrastination. Students get untracked and begin developing momentum; my involvement in their work increases. Here is the handout I give to students:

Research Design for the Multigenre Research Paper

A "research design" jump-starts your paper, gets you thinking about your topic in a concentrated way. You'll do some initial exploration with words on paper. You'll come to think things you would not have had you only mused about your topic. I also want you to get to the library and Internet early so you find out what information and resources are available.

The research design must be typed. It can be single-spaced. Make the margins spacious enough so I can write comments in them and suggest further resources. This assignment is worth 5% of your course grade.

Parts of Your Multigenre Research Design

1. Name your topic.
2. Describe what you know about your topic (Without consulting anything, go to the keyboard and freewrite what you already know. Let it sit a day or so, then reread, refining for specificity and editing for redundancies). If you want, you can do this as bullets.
3. Tell what you want to learn about (Remember Curious George? You be Curious Student).
4. Describe the origins of your research. What sparked your interest in the topic? Why do you want to know more about it? (This is just me being nosey, being Curious Tom.)
5. List at least a *dozen* questions you have about your topic (or twenty, or fifty).
6. Describe your plan for collecting information about your topic.
7. Provide a preliminary bibliography (Don't bail out here. Get a sense of what is out there. I expect this to be thorough).

Chelsea decided to write her multigenre paper about eating disorders, which required her to look intensively both outward and inward. Here is her research design:

Chelsea Donovan

EDT 180

I'm eager to see you put your mind to this topic, Chelsea. Combine the intellectual insights you gain with your personal experience and fierce will, and I think you will produce a moving, fulfilling and informative multigenre paper.

Your preliminary bibliography is thin. I want to see you search out more sources. Maybe even look into female adolescent psychology in general. Seek out some qualitative research done by doctors. I'll bet you'll find interesting profiles and interviews with people who suffer eating disorders.

MGP Research Design

1. My Topic

   The topic that I want to concentrate on for my multigenre research paper is eating disorders. I want to explore the root problems of eating disorders, since eating disorders are commonly a symptom to larger problems. I want to explore not only the physical aspects of the disorder, but also, mostly, the mindset of the disorder. I'd also like to know how these disorders affect the people that surround the person suffering from the disorder.

2. What I Already Know

   I know that ten percent of college-aged girls suffer from eating disorders. Although, I suspect that number is probably deflated since I would imagine that many body image issues go untreated or are dealt with privately. I know that there are many types of eating disorders that are normally defined by the physical means that they display. Anorexia, bulimia/purging, and compulsive eating are the most recognized kinds of eating disorders. These definitions do not fully encompass all kinds and severities of eating disorders, though, so some get called "unspecified".

   What I know about the mindset of eating disorders comes from my own experiences with my relationship with food, eating, and body image. I have struggled alternately with E.D. tendencies and full blown, extended periods of restricting and losing weight. I am aware that my experiences do not encompass all of the different ways that people suffer from these disorders, and they certainly are not as extreme as some cases, but they do give me a certain empathy and understanding for even the sickest of sufferers. I know that eating disorders sometimes get looked at as vanity or selfishness, but the truth is that the problems go so much deeper. The issues stem from a need for control, negative self-image, and feelings of self-worthlessness.

I hope you can shed light on this. The second multigenre paper I read about a young woman with ED, I learned so much. As she delved into the reasons she was coming to understand about the disease, I found myself resisting, not understanding how someone so bright and attractive could be suffering so. Maybe you can get at some of these psychological reasons.

3. What I Want To Learn

Since I have some idea what goes on in the mindset of the disordered (a word that always makes me laugh a little because I can only imagine Amelia Bedelia taking that statement literally and organizing all of the food on my plate), I would like to learn more about how it affects the people around that person. Especially when a person is really sick and refusing treatment, I wonder how that affects the friends and family. How many people stick around and fight the disease with that person? I think a lot of people see eating disorders as self-inflicted punishment or a choice, instead of the disease and disorder that it is.

I would also like to find out how many girls out there struggle silently. I would like to know what they think the reason is for their eating disorder. Also, I would like to explore why people refuse treatment.

4. The Origins of My Research

The origins of my research probably officially began my freshman year of college when I started obsessively searching for ways to lose weight. I was constantly reading online about recipes and work out plans that would help me lose weight. All the while, I was restricting my food intake and feeling sick with myself for anything that I put into my stomach. The origins for my research reached a climax a couple summers ago when, after getting sick at a party I attended, I realized that I may have found a way to start purging and I tried a few more times that summer.

Eventually, my logical side always wins out against my eating disorder tendencies. After a while, my mind forces me to stop the unhealthy behavior because I am smart enough to know it is wrong and life threateningly unhealthy. I know a lot of the physical issues that can come out of starving yourself, purging, and using laxatives. I value my life enough not to destroy it permanently. But, I want to explore why other people don't stop. Why the eating disorder wins out above their own life and health.

I originally was not going to use this as a topic for my multi-genre paper. It felt too big and too close to home. I'm hoping that writing about it and researching it will help me in my own process

You could write a satiric piece about Amelia organizing food.

How do boyfriends typically react to the disease. Do they stick around?

Maybe you can find books that feature interviews with people with ED.

This is probably an important scene to dramatize, to capture the emotional and physical description of this act—your sudden realization.

This is quite a statement, Chelsea. It seems to obviously be true. But there are things keeping many from seeing it.

of healing. That facing it head on will help me finally end my battle with my body.

5. Questions for my research

    a. How many people suffer from eating disorders? Is there a projected number of people who suffer silently?

    b. What is the most common eating disorder?

    c. How do you recognize an eating disorder in yourself or others?

    d. What is some of the psychology behind disordered eating?

    e. How are friends and family affected by eating disorders?

    f. Is there a certain profile of a person with an eating disorder?

    g. Why do people do things to their body when they know they are unhealthy?

    h. Why do people refuse treatment?

    i. What kind of treatment is out there?

    j. How does a person's relationship with food and their body affect other aspects of their life?

    k. Why do people decide to deal with this silently?

    l. Why is food and how much you eat or don't eat such a stigmatized and avoided subject?

    m. How does outside media affect self image?

    n. How much education are young women and men really getting about a healthy eating and healthy body image?

    o. How do people get information about eating disorders?

    p. What are the bigger problems of which eating disorders are a symptom?

6. My Research Plan

    I plan to begin my research by finding the answers to some of the questions I have. I want to look at some personal stories and accounts of people who have struggled with eating disorders. As well as get some accounts of the family and friends that surround a person with an eating disorder. I know what my experience is, and I plan to bring that experience into my writing, but I also want to know as much as I can about other people's experiences. I also plan on researching the kind of treatment that a person can

I'll bet there are subtle hints that would go unnoticed if you are not looking for them.

Why doesn't gaining maturity help in every case? You know, the adolescent brain developing greater powers of cognition.

This would be a huge list of things people do to their bodies that they know are unhealthy. Think of smokers. When I was a kid the vast majority of adults smoked.

Be great if you could conduct a focus group with young women who battle ED.

get for eating disorders. In order to get both points of view, I want to research the sites and books that are put in place to get people healthy and also research the sites, books, and media that help people become unhealthy. I have heard about websites called "pro-ana" sites. It stands for pro-anorexia, and they are websites that people create in order to connect to other people who use anorexia as a lifestyle. These websites use the word Anna to stand for anorexia and they portray Anna as a girl who gives suggestions and advice that help connect and extend the eating disorder. I have also run into websites during my research that are called "thinspiration" sites. They are sites that show pictures of girls who are unhealthily skinny to serve as inspiration for girls trying to lose weight. Some of these websites are disturbingly surprising and give insight into how much a disease this actually is.

7. Preliminary Bibliography

"The BEATRICE Interview: 1998." *Beatrice.com.* 1998. 16 Mar. 2011 <www.beatrice.com/interviews/hornbacher/>.

Eating Disorders | Anorexia | Bulimia | Binge Eating Disorder | Compulsive Overeating | The Something Fishy Website on Eating Disorders. 16 Mar. 2011 <www.something-fishy.org/>.

Lamott, Anne. "My Secret Body." Salon.com - Salon.com. 16 Mar. 2011 <www.salon.com/april97/columnists/lamott970410 .html>.

Rhodes, Constance. Life inside the "thin" cage: a personal look into the hidden world of the chronic dieter. Colorado Springs, CO: Shaw Books, 2003.

Terrific you found a Lamott piece, considering how much you liked Bird By Bird.

Immersion in this multigenre project will teach students about writing, but also about thinking: the benefits of perseverance, the synergistic qualities of deep, sustained thinking over time that makes for abundance—one idea leading to reconceptualization, one genre sparking another. Immersion will teach students to pay attention. It will teach them how sometimes ideas and solutions to problems come when we aren't consciously paying attention, when we're relaxing or otherwise occupied, maybe running, swimming, or walking, and that wonderful right hemisphere is doing the good work of composting information and sifting through it, making connections and suddenly a burst of insight arrives from seemingly out of the blue when it actually came from Carrie's grey matter. The research design gets that process started.

14

Memo for a
Final Boost

TO: MULTIGENRE WRITERS
From: Romano
Date: After Reading Your Research Designs
Re: The Research Process

I am invigorated by the research directions you've mapped out. What diversity of topics! Some personal, some idiosyncratic, some whimsical, some serious, all intriguing, worthy, and rich with possibility. Now you need only bring your good minds and strong work ethic to the quest. I'll accompany you on your research journeys, seeking to be helpful, marveling at the sights, pointing out anything that might be useful, quickening to your learning and revelations.

You've pushed forward your thinking by generating questions about your topics. You have in mind information you want to know. That's an excellent start, but don't be settled. By the Gods of Inquiry!— remain open to questions and connections that flame up in you *after* you've begun your research. (The new questions, curiosities, and connections could not have occurred *until* you learned more about your topics. You'd have asked them before had you known more.)

Some research advice, humbly offered:

Value your previous thinking and experience. Use it if it seems helpful to understanding and communicating. I once researched collaborative learning. I learned about its roots, why it worked, when it didn't, how achievement that appeared to be individual was actually, in fundamental ways, collaborative. The professor, in passing, mentioned Walt Whitman, a writer I admired. I'd had a long history with Whitman since I was nineteen. A few years earlier, I'd read *Walt Whitman: A Life* (Kaplan 1980). Whitman was that quintessential American voice who broke open the doors of free verse poetry in America and seemed a self-made, indomitable *I*. Justin Kaplan synthesized how Whitman had been influenced, shaped, and inspired by the intellectual ferment, culture, and teeming life of New York City in the mid-nineteenth century. No *Mannahatta*, no Walt Whitman as we've come to know him. I ended up writing about Whitman for the lead of the paper, and then, twenty-five pages later, coming back to the poet in the concluding paragraphs. That serendipitous comment by the professor turned out to be synergistic. So be alert to everything. Let nothing be lost on you.

Read deeply. Gather information and gain understanding from the articles, books, and online sources you've cited in your preliminary bibliography. The key word, however, is *preliminary*. Follow clues you find in your reading. Those can lead you to even more relevant research. If an author cites another author's work that looks promising, pursue the reference. Riches may lie there. Example: As a master's degree student many years ago, I was charged in one class with critiquing the research paper of one of my peers. When I read her paper about Hemingway's *Green Hills of Africa* (1935), I noticed that she cited an article written by one of the professors in the English department, a man I knew through his teenagers who babysat our daughter. I sought out the article, which proved an invigorating read, synthesizing much thinking about Hemingway's African memoir (what I think of now as an early example of creative nonfiction by one of the prose master's of the twentieth century). Also—and I needed this as a new grad student seeking my own academic written voice—Professor Reardon's essay, in its clarity, strong sense of personal voice, and lucid delivery of surprising information and insights, modeled how an academic essay might be written. So be a detective. Look for relevancy everywhere.

Seek primary source material when you can. Try conducting interviews with people knowledgeable about your topic. Before the interview, prepare clear questions you can ask the interviewee. Then, in the heat of the interview, listen. Be alert. Jot notes. Gather more information than you can use. When an explanation is general or complicated, ask the interviewee to say more, clarify a point, provide an example. Get direct quotes; they will enliven your writing. When you are not sure you have gotten a quote accurately, stop for a moment, say, "Tell me if I have this right" and then read aloud what you have written. This communicates how much you value your interviewee's point of view, how you are striving for accuracy and fairness. It also gives your subject a chance to elaborate.

Try writing *verbatim accounts*. Years ago, I learned about these from Don Graves, the great teacher and researcher of children's literacy at the University of New Hampshire. A "verbatim account" is a detailed description of everything you can remember about an event, encounter, or interview that you *write as soon as you can after it has occurred*. Be excruciatingly detailed. You'll be amazed how much information, perceptions, and inferences you retrieve that would have been lost to you had you waited to write. Language leads to thinking. Thinking activates memory, which triggers more language, more visualization, more thinking. Riches unfold in verbatim accounts.

When I wrote a memoir (Romano 2008), a few chapters were easier to write than others because years earlier—thirty-one years earlier in one case—I had written in my notebook what were essentially verbatim accounts of significant encounters fraught with emotion and drama. In the notebook entries I hadn't *told* what emotions I felt. Rather, and much more valuable to me, I'd described in detail where we were, what happened, what was said, and what I thought. I'd tried to accurately and exhaustively remember all the dialog. The more I retrieved, the more I remembered. The more I reconstructed the dialog, the more dialog came back to me. These notebook entries became primary source material for the memoir.

Lastly, may the work you're embarking upon carry you away, land you in the zone, send you blissfully lost in literacy. The psychologist, Mihaly Csikszentmihalyi, described the state of mind I'm talking about in *Flow: The Psychology of Optimal Experience* (1990):

> a sense that one's skills are adequate to cope with the challenges at hand, in a goal-directed, rule-bound action system that provides clear clues as to how well one is performing. Concentration is so intense that there is no attention left over to think about anything irrelevant, or to worry about problems. Self-consciousness disappears, and the sense of time becomes distorted. An activity that produces such experience is so

gratifying that people are willing to do it for its own sake, with little concern for what they will get out of it, even when it is difficult, or dangerous. (1990, 71)

The state of flow can happen while eating, cooking, gardening, gaming, bicycling, gambling, watching a movie, making love, teaching, reading, writing, conversing—any activity that we develop a knack for, perform well, but are challenged by, keeping us on our toes so boredom stays at bay. I know it might be hard to imagine you could get so involved in a research project that time falls away and absorption and fulfillment become one, as spurts of serotonin drive you on to gather fascinating information and make striking connections. As an adult, I've found such intellectual engagement the closest I've come to stabbing a grounder blazing down the third base line and throwing a strike to first.

Your research and multigenre writing with its freedom, choice, and discipline has the potential for optimal psychological experience. Give it a try. Let yourself go. You've picked a topic of consuming interest, something you are passionate about. Ride this. You very well might find yourself online in the early morning hours, staying awake much later than you intended. You might be engrossed in a book at the library when the lights flicker, signaling closing time. You might be writing one genre for your paper and in rapid succession jot in the margin notes for other genres you could write. If such things happen, you'll be in multigenre heaven right here on earth.

> "This research project was simultaneously draining and invigorating. I knew very little about my topic to begin with and felt very limited in my genres. Once I started researching—POW!—the possibilities kept coming."
>
> Matt Alander, teacher

SECTION

III

What to Write, How to Write It

Once students start writing multiple genres, their well of creativity does not run dry. The more they write, the more they think of to write. This section provides specific strategies to help students discover fertile writing territories within their topics, the "What to Write." The "How to Write It" contains suggestions for invigorating ideas of narrative, exposition, poetry, and experimental writing.

15

What to Write About

GET TO THE HEART. GET TO THE TANGIBLE. FORGET ABOUT telling how you feel. Forget about big ideas and abstract concepts. Don't write about how dedicated Sam was to writing, how she would sacrifice much in order to get the writing done. Instead, write that scene of a North Carolina morning, still dark at 4:00 a.m. when Sam swings her feet over the edge of the bed, rises, brews coffee, and—still in her pajamas—sits cross-legged on the couch, writing in her notebook, coming more awake as words quicken her mind, pausing now and then to sip black coffee, before showering and heading for her teaching job.

When students are well into their inquiry, I ask them to take inventory. I place these categories on the white board: important things, meaningful places, crucial people, central acts/processes, memorable conversations. I give students time to think about their topics and gather what fits into these categories, using the brainstorming activity as an archeological tool to unearth information. In this way, I gently prod students to identify and talk about specificities. For example, a multigenre project about Bram Stoker's *Dracula*:

- important things (garlic, crucifix, wooden stake, bat, sunlight, coffin, severed head, prominent incisors, time)

- meaningful places (Castle Dracula, Transylvania, London, Carfax Abbey, Renfield's mad mind)

- crucial people (Harker, Mina, Lucy, Renfield, Dr. Van Helsing, Vlad the Impaler, Dracula's first victim)

- central acts/processes (sucking blood, moving to London, procedure for destroying a vampire, Dracula's transformation into bat, wolf, mist)

- memorable conversations (first conversation between Dracula and Van Helsing, Dracula's job interview with a Starbucks' manager—the Count preferred to work the nightshift)

This laying out of specific territories provides writers with possible topics to write about throughout the multigenre process. They can come back to it repeatedly and add to the categories as they learn and think. I know that writing about these specific topics, bringing them to vividness with imagery and detail and dialog, will deepen the writer's understanding and spark further thinking. The writing leads to more writing, more genres, more insights. It's the principle of the myelin sheath that insulates nerve fibers in our bodies. The more we perform actions, whether its hitting golf balls out of sand traps, baking pies, learning to walk for toddlers, the more that a substance called myelin wraps the nerve fibers involved in the activity. The more the nerve fibers are wrapped, the better insulated they are. The better insulated they are, the faster and more efficiently they send electrical signals (Coyle 2009). Performance is enhanced. Exercise increases the capacity for exercise. Breastfeeding stimulates the production of milk. Abundance makes for abundance. That's how multigenre works.

Indelible Moments

The categories I provide won't bring to consciousness all possibilities for productive writing, so I also ask students to identify "indelible moments" in their topics (Romano 2000, 123). Indelible moments bear paying attention to when you write anything: a commentary, a poem, a description, even a literary essay. (What image from the novel sticks in your mind like an indelible stain? Santiago stabbing sharks with the knife lashed to the oar? Scout standing on the Radley porch looking at the neighborhood from the point of view that Boo did each day? That grasshopper landing on Mary Oliver's hand?)

Writes one of my undergraduate students,

Indelible moments remind me of what my dad and I call *a day of days*, a day that is somehow so special, unique, or meaningful that it stands out among other days. Just one event, one encounter, one feeling can make a moment indelible. It doesn't have to be pretty. Sometimes what sticks with me is meaningful because it's ugly. And that's okay. In fact, it's necessary. I think it's important that the multigenre paper sustains itself as an honest portrayal of your topic.

Holly Jeric, college junior

Indelible moments persist for a reason. They're often representative of big emotion and complex meaning. Indelible moments can be defining. In the opening chapter, I cited Brian, my former high school student who had written a multigenre paper about John Lennon. He began with the indelible image he'd imagined many times, even though he hadn't witnessed it: the moment of Lennon's murder. Sometimes we know what the indelible moments mean; sometimes we must render them in writing to find out.

Through research, we can inform our imaginations to enhance our understanding, our empathy, our conception of some aspect of our topics. What might a particular scene have looked and sounded and felt like? What do I need to learn in order to vividly render that indelible moment? I remember reading an interview with Alex Haley soon after *Roots* (1976) was published. Haley spoke about his ancestor— Kunta Kinte, "the African" who became Toby. When he was apprehended the final time after escaping the plantation, the slave hunters tied him to a tree. So he could never run again, they chopped off half of one of his feet.

The weight of that indelible moment pressed upon Haley. He knew he had to write about it. To imagine the heinous act more fully, he read about the biology of the foot, the bones, muscles, tendons, nerves, blood vessels. He imagined the violence done to them when the axe plunged through to the ground. He rendered that scene to sear it into readers' minds as it had been seared into his.

Indelible moments can be written briefly and powerfully, as Brian did in his opening poem that rendered John Lennon's assassination. Or they can be more fully developed. Below is a narrative from my life sparked by an indelible moment:

When I was a high school junior, I tried to sit in the last seat of the row by the windows in English class. The teacher had taught me the year before and knew my ways. She made me sit in the first seat of the middle row, directly in front of her desk. Although my vision of the rest of the class was limited, I was privy to everything that happened at Mrs. Dunbar's desk.

One morning we were constructing formal outlines for a classification paper. Mrs. Dunbar had grudgingly granted us a day to work in class provided we not "fiddle around." I sat at my desk drawing diagrams of imaginary football plays. At the top of my paper was the single word: *Sports*. I was fiddling around.

From the back of the room, I heard footsteps. Before I could turn my head to see who it was, Bill Jackson brushed by my desk. Bill was beautifully built, the best athlete in school, a straight A student, polite, and black. He always said, "Yes, Ma'am" and "No, Ma'am," which made Mrs. Dunbar glow. I'd known Bill all my life. Hundreds of times since we'd been freshmen I'd pressed footballs against his muscular stomach and silently wished him good running as he plunged toward a hole in the line of scrimmage.

Bill stood by Mrs. Dunbar's desk. He wore his white cardigan sweater that featured on one pocket a large green letter "M" he'd earned his sophomore year as starting left halfback.

"Oh, music," said Mrs. Dunbar, taking Bill's outline. "I love music. Mr. Dunbar and I go dancing at least twice a month at the Turquoise Ballroom."

"Yes, Ma'am," said Bill. "I'm a music lover, too."

"Let's see, your classifications are folk, classical, jazz . . . good, I love Benny Goodman . . . and you have country and western, and rock-'n'—"

Mrs. Dunbar's face flushed. Her voice lost its lilt.

Bill looked puzzled. "Rock-'n'-roll?" he asked. "Is there something wrong?"

Mrs. Dunbar pinched the outline with thumb and forefinger. She closed her eyes and swung the paper over to Bill. "It's trash," she said.

"Rock-'n'-roll?"

"It's trash."

"I'm not saying it's good or bad," said Bill. "I'm just classifying it as a form of music."

"If there is one thing rock-'n'-roll is not," said Mrs. Dunbar, "it's music."

Bill looked like he might protest further, but he was silent, holding the outline he'd meticulously completed.

"Either drop rock-'n'-roll as a category or choose a new topic."

Bill swallowed, still recovering, I think, from this unexpected ambush when he thought he'd entered friendly territory.

Mrs. Dunbar gazed straight above my head to the back wall of the classroom.

Bill wavered a moment longer, then grimaced, "Yes, Ma'am."

I lowered my eyes and looked at the play I'd created on paper, imagined it with real players on a green football field under bright lights. Amidst a flurry of movement, I handed our left halfback the ball. He sprinted toward the sideline and cut downfield for what I knew would be a touchdown.

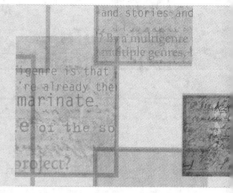

Explain to students the concept of indelible moments, which are nearly always attached to vivid images. Discuss moments from literature you've read together that are indelibly etched in memory. Tell about indelible moments from your own life. Move students to discuss indelible images from their lives. Emphasize a moment, an image, a brief span of time. Ask students to focus on their topic and retrieve as many indelible moments as they can. Have them choose a moment and render it in detail.

16

Don't Run from Exposition

IN THIS PROJECT THAT COMPELS WRITERS TO AVAIL THEM-selves of the big world mural of genres, subgenres, hybrid genres, and all possibilities that narrative thinking offers, I make students write exposition—at least one piece of informational or persuasive writing, 250–350 words. Any single piece longer than that threatens to stop the flow, the movement, the varietal nature of multigenre.

I want the exposition to serve a purpose, of course, not just be included to fulfill my requirement. One first-year college student wrote about the building of America's interstate highway system in the late 1950s. At the very beginning of his paper, Stephen saw the need to tell readers "*How We Got Here*," the *Here* being the point at which President Eisenhower signed the Federal Highway Act on June 29, 1956. In an accessible informational piece, readers learn, to their surprise, that there had been other attempts to build interstate highways over the previous thirty years. Those had been sidetracked by bureaucrats or abandoned because of World War II—useful information for readers to have in their heads before immersion in the multiplicity of genres.

Anne wrote a multigenre paper based upon a book that had piqued her interest: *Loving Frank* by Nancy Horan (2007). Since the book concentrated on one aspect of the life of Frank Lloyd Wright—the love affair with Mamah Borthwick—Anne thought she needed to remind readers of something. She accompanied her exposition with a photograph of "Falling Water," in Bear Run, Pennsylvania. She provides an epigram before her exposition:

The reality of the house is order
The blessing of the house is community
The glory of the house is hospitality
The crown of the house is godliness

Frank Lloyd Wright, 1905 (inscribed on the fireplace of the Heath House)

Loving Frank's Legacy

Frank Lloyd Wright became one of the few world renowned architects during his lifetime. From the early work of Prairie homes to the construction of the controversial design that is the Guggenheim museum, Wright showed a true gift for creativity and innovation. Although *Loving Frank* by Nancy Horan, concentrates on the love affair with Mamah Borthwick Cheney, his real claim to fame was the incredible pieces of art he created through architecture.

Wright began his architectural career learning from J. Lyman Silsbee. After a large fire in Chicago, Silsbee was in great demand. Wright soon left Silsbee, claiming to be uninspired and signed a five year contract with Alder and Sullivan. After gaining knowledge from Sullivan, or "beloved master" as he called him, Wright began to take on smaller domestic projects, which were based on his idea of organic architecture.

For Wright, organic architecture meant "buildings [homes mostly] that adhered to the law of nature and that, through their design and their use of indigenous materials, were tied to the native landscape" (Drennan 38). His houses "grew naturally out of the needs of the client, the nature of the site, and the kinds of native materials that were available" (Middleton 18). His home, Taliesin, located in Wisconsin, was built with this mindset.

Wright not only designed houses, but also many notable buildings around the world. Completed in 1922, he designed and built the Imperial Hotel in Tokyo, Japan, which stood until 1968. In 1936 he built "Falling Water" in Pennsylvania, one of the most well known houses and now a national monument, which can still be visited today. Wright also designed the Solomon R. Guggenheim museum, completed in 1959.

Loving Frank gives the inside look at an aspect of Frank Lloyd Wright's love affair, but it is important to remember that through the controversy of the relationship, a truly talented and gifted man was creating magnificent art that changed the world of architecture forever.

Anne Jaworski, college junior

For her expository piece, second-year student Ali Cesta wasn't concerned with providing backstory or with reminding readers of a critical aspect of her subject so they would avoid a distorted picture. Ali had a different purpose. She investigated infidelity, its history, psychology, and consequences. Her exposition is marked by her sharp tongue, acerbic sense of humor, jaded point of view, and irrepressible voice:

Infidelity can be defined in many different ways, from a simple glance to a torrid love affair. The fact is it's everywhere. Approximately 45–60% of men cheat sometime during marriage, closely trailed by 25–40% of women. Unfaithfulness has been around forever.

> *If you talk in your sleep, don't mention my name. If you walk in your sleep, forget where you came.*
> ELVIS PRESLEY

In the *Bible*, Jacob married two women; David slept with Uriah the Hittite's wife, impregnated her, and then sent Uriah into battle to be killed. Classy stuff. In Greek mythology, the affair of Helen of Troy and Paris was the cause of the Trojan War.

More than a few of our great leaders have been unfaithful. George Washington was known to have had many affairs; Jefferson knocked up one of his slaves; Cleveland admitted to having an illegitimate child; Harding used to sleep with women in a White House closet; Eisenhower had a wartime affair; JFK slept with damn near everyone; Johnson had a child with his mistress; and we all know Clinton's story.

> *An affair has more rules than a marriage.*
> THE GOOD GERMAN

Martin Luther King Jr., one of the most respected and honorable men ever to live, was caught by the FBI having an "encounter" with someone who most certainly was not his wife.

I don't believe in cheating, but I believe it happens, and it happens a lot. Over 70% of affairs begin in the workplace. Devices have been created specifically to spy on spouses or partners to see if they're cheating. Someone could buy a voice recorder for around fifty dollars, install it into a car or around the house, and listen to everything their partner says. For a few more pretty pennies, a phone tap can be installed and will record up to thirty-five hours of telephone conversation. Then there is, of course, the infamous GPS. A GPS tracking device is easily installed into cars, and a spouse can know

> *One doesn't kiss in the marketplace as one kisses in the forest.*
> THE SCARLET LETTER

where you are and when you were there. A word to the wise: if you're going to cheat, take a look around before you go gallivanting about with your lover. Oh, and don't be a dumbass.

Ali Cesta, college sophomore

I require students to include at least one piece of expository writing in their multigenre papers because most of them, otherwise, run from that genre. Since entering high school, many of them have been expositioned to death. Most of that writing was about literature, and more often than not, in expositions of five-you-know-whats. I won't even call this formulaic subgenre an essay, a word derived from the French *essai*, which was coined by Michel de Montaigne in the sixteenth century "from essayer, to attempt" (Moffett 1983, 171). The spirit of essay, then, is to explore, to discover, to try to reach personal truth. Moffett goes on to assert that "English literature has maintained a marvelous tradition [of the essay], fusing personal experience, private vision, and downright eccentricity, with intellectual rigor and verbal objectification. In color, depth, and stylistic originality it rivals some of our best poetry" (Moffett 1983, 171).

I hate what has happened to exposition in the minds of many students in American schools. Most of the writing I do is expository. I find it a genre in which I can be creative, urgent, limber, provocative, exploratory, linguistically sophisticated, and voiceful, using all I know about making writing vivid: imagery, strong verbs, directness, surprise, figurative language, convincing logic, rhythmical syntax, and stories.

I am reminded of this every time I run across a piece of beautiful, expository writing, simple and exquisite. Every morning I experience the electronic version of Garrison Keillor's "The Writer's Almanac." In addition to reading a poem each day, Keillor reads brief expository pieces about a notable person's birthday or significant anniversary. These short pieces themselves are lucid, succinct, direct, informative examples of expository writing. On the birthday of Carl Sagan, Keillor spoke about the astronomer's efforts to see that spacecraft were equipped with cameras:

Sagan also persuaded NASA engineers to turn the Voyager I spacecraft around on Valentine's Day in 1990, so that it could take a picture of Earth from the very edge of our solar system, about 4 billion miles away. In the photograph, Earth appears as a tiny bluish speck. Sagan later wrote of the photograph, "Look again at that dot. That's here. That's home. That's us. On it everyone you love, everyone you know, everyone you ever heard of, every human being who ever was, lived out their lives . . . [on] a mote of dust suspended in a sunbeam." (Keillor 2011)

Give me all of that kind of writing you have, both Keillor's clear, informative lead-in to contextualize what's coming and Sagan's short sentences, parallel structure, and final vivid image. The passage is explanatory and descriptive as it seeks to convince you of the marvel of this life on earth.

Something I remember about writing a multigenre paper is the importance of the little stories and the way they mesh and meld to say something bigger.

Holly Jeric, college junior

Crafting Narrative

Story carries the multigenre load. Not exposition. Not even poetry. That work is done by story, tale telling. Multigenre wants more than understanding, more than consideration of an argument, more than a calculation of loss. Multigenre wants readers to see, to participate, to experience. Through story, we visualize characters and their actions, are aroused by twists of plot, feel life played out through the sensory language of narrative.

But all storytelling is not created equal. You know effective storytellers. I certainly do. Garrison Keillor on Minnesota Public Radio's "Prairie Home Companion" tells engaging stories about his fictional town, Lake Wobegon. The great children's literacy scholar, Donald Graves, was another great storyteller. Thomas Newkirk writes movingly of Don's ability to weave tales. At large conferences

> a packed audience would respond enthusiastically to his humor, his stories of children in his study, his description of their writing, and his ability to mimic conversations with these children. At times, these stories had the weight of parables. (Newkirk 2009, 125)

And we all knew great storytellers from our youth. For me that great storyteller was my uncle, Gigi Chiavari, who came to America in 1913 when he was eighteen years old. Uncle Gigi was hard to understand until you caught up with the rhythms of his thick Italian accent. But could he ever tell stories . . . he told them with his entire body. His facial expressions revealed the emotion of his words. He punctuated meaning with hand and arm gestures. He sometimes engaged kinesthetic intelligence by acting out what he described. It was not uncommon to see Uncle Gigi on hands and knees or dancing about the room or riding an imaginary horse or looking fearfully over his shoulder—whatever the story required. His sense of humor was quick, and his eye for detail sharp. This Italian immigrant with little formal education in the old country, knew intuitively how to end a story with a payoff.[1]

We all know bad storytellers, too. People who provide too little detail, no proper context, and deliver the payoff in the beginning instead of the end. And we know the opposite: People who have us rolling our eyes and searching for ways to break into their monologs, although we can rarely find an opening to wedge into the unrelenting stream of unfiltered words full of tangents, didactic points, and condescending questions that raise our blood pressure.

Such people don't know how to craft a story. How to create characters with dialog and description. How to make a setting come alive with just the right details. How to reveal conflict, build tension, and lead listeners to a release, a payoff, a pleasurable denouement that is clear and satisfying. They don't know how to understate, how to trust readers to make meaning through the information being delivered. They don't know how to be subtle yet emphatically implicit.

Here's an example of a well-written story that came in an email message from a friend. The storyteller crafts language so readers see characters and hear them speak. She lets action reveal plot. She lets us be surprised the way she was. Lastly, she is emphatically implicit with a final, telling detail:

> I was at the bank getting a money order for the cash that was donated to the DNC Saturday night. The teller counted the money three times and then started to run the money order.
>
> "Do you want to just write in the name on the 'to' line?" she asked.
>
> "I'd rather have the name typed on the money order."
>
> She got the form in the printer and asked who it should be made out to.
>
> "The Democratic National Committee," I told her.
>
> She typed D-E-M, then looked at me with one of those "I need help" kinds of looks. I finished spelling the word for her.

---

[1] For getting effective aspects of oral expression into writing see Chapter 42 of *Crafting Authentic Voice* (Romano 2004).

"Oh, yeah, that's right," she said.

She typed out "National" just fine, then asked, "Does committee have one 'm' or two?"

"Two," I told her.

She finished typing the money order, pulled it out of the printer, and handed it to me with the proud smile of a tough job finally accomplished. As I walked away from the teller window, I glanced down at the money order made out to the "Democratic National Commity."

Phyllis Mendenhall, Chief Advisor
Department of Teacher Education
Miami University

The nature of multigenre is many. One genre cannot oppressively dominate or the paper loses balance and variety. A narrative or exposition of a thousand words knocks the entire paper out of whack, disrupts the flow, the rhythm, the feeling of accomplishment in moving from one genre to the next as we accumulate information and build meaning. Shorter stories are more effective than longer ones. The concept of flash fiction is particularly valuable to the multigenre writer.

Miniature tales, revealing anecdotes, very short stories—narratives that happen in a *flash*—have been popular for years. The authors of *Flash Fiction* (Thomas, Thomas, and Hazuka 1992) hold that *flashes*, as they are often called, run between 250 and 750 words, long enough to indicate character, build plot, and deliver a denouement that might be surprising or troubling or sweetly ambiguous. The authors are quick to point out that the success of flashes does not depend upon length, but upon their "depth, their clarity of vision, their human significance—the extent to which the reader is able to recognize in them the real stuff of real life" (Thomas, Thomas, and Hazuka 1992, 12).

In an explanation of flash fiction, Robert Olen Butler notes that

a human being (or a "character") cannot exist for even a few seconds of time on planet Earth without desiring something. Yearning for something, a word I prefer because it suggests the deepest level of desire, where literature strives to go. Fiction is the art form of human yearning, no matter how long or short that work of fiction is. (Butler 2009, 102)

When a character's yearning is challenged, blocked, or thwarted, you have "the essence of plot" (Butler 2009, 103). An example: Charlene Kohn, a primary multiage teacher when I met her one summer in my multigenre course at the University of New Hampshire, wrote a multigenre paper titled "Threads." In a succinct introduction, she explored and revealed the "community of relatives who sewed and taught me their art." They gave Charlene "the gift of needle and thread." When she began her exploration of "the enormous genre of needlework," Charlene found herself writing about the human relationships and stories of this passion she'd followed for so many years: the joys, conflicts, hurts, and triumphs. You'll recognize the yearning in the 334 word flash (non)fiction.

Treasure Lost

I'm sitting here on the front porch of my Great Grandma Clara's house. It's a hot June day in Kansas and I'm trying so hard to hear some information and see what is going on inside. I know she is dead. I know I can help them sort through her things, deciding who gets what. I am not allowed in. I'm the one who gets to watch the little kids while they are playing in the yard. They are too young to understand. I'm ten and I know.

Daddy said the job of the day is deciding who gets what. Daddy and Aunt Harriette are in charge of separating all Grandma's belongings into piles. That's what they're doing right now. I heard them talking last night, so I know. I heard Aunt Harriette say that each of us great grandkids should get one special thing to treasure. One thing.

I told Daddy I wanted Grandma's thimble. Then I told Aunt Harriette. This morning I even told Mom. I know right where it is. I could run up the stairs and reach into Grandma's sewing basket and grab it. It would only take a minute. I wish they would let me inside, just for one tiny minute. But, they won't. Two whole days like this! Babysitting and waiting and thinking about that little silver thimble that Grandma always wears on her finger when she sews.

Daddy is coming through the door, there's something small in his hand. My heart jumps and my stomach bubbles: he remembered!

"Aunt Harriette and I decided you should have this. It was very special to Grandma and it will help you to remember her." He handed me an object I had never seen before. So, this is my treasure? I think to myself.

The one thing that will keep Grandma alive for me? My lip begins to quiver and Daddy hugs me. "It will be all right," he says. But he doesn't understand. I look at the cameo and cry.

Charlene Kohn, teacher

In all the years I've been teaching multigenre, "Threads" has been the most artfully designed. Charlene used a heavy weight off-white paper, the twenty-seven pages hand stitched on the left. The written genres on many pages were accompanied by patches of fabric, a crocheted flower, a photograph, a color drawing. Across the first page runs a heavy string from left to right that we don't see again until the final page when it resumes its journey, as though it had run through the entire paper. One page features an envelope; inside it are "tools of the trade": miniature scissors, a safety pin, buttons, a tape measure, and straight pins.

And holding this multigenre paper together is story: flashes, narrative poems, character sketches, anecdotes, a dream narrative.

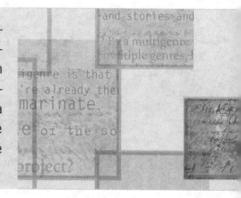

Push students to find the stories in their topics. What are characters' yearnings? What steps are taken to achieve them? What obstacles stand in the way? What are the consequences? Try first-person point of view, even if that means stepping into the shoes of a character outside the self. Try third-person point of view, even with a story they have personally lived, this to make the familiar a little less so as they write. Try second-person point of view and fly in the face of decades of formal writing purists.

18

Quality Writing

ONE OF MY STUDENTS LEANED HER HEAD INTO MY OFFICE.

"I've got a book for you," LaTia said.

I looked up from my desk. "Yeah?" My facial expression was receptive: eyebrows raised, slight smile, curious demeanor. Inside, however, I was rolling my eyes. Someone else with a book I should read? I have a stack of books I should read!

"It's right up your alley," LaTia said.

My alley, I thought, is so cluttered with books it's impassable.

"You'll love this." She stepped inside and extended the book, a slim, battered paperback, the pages dog-eared, the cover stained and crinkled.

"My high school English teacher introduced us to it."

The book, I must report, became part of my teaching repertoire soon after I read it. I was chagrined by the publication date. How had twenty years gone by without my learning of J. Ruth Gendler's *The Book of Qualities* (1984)? How could friends not have recommended it until now, until LaTia, bless her, handed me her precious copy?

Gendler identifies ninety-nine "qualities." Sometimes the quality is an emotion or a feeling, like Anxiety, Longing, Ambivalence, Joy, Jealousy, Anger. Sometimes the quality is a concept or thing, like Pain, Intelligence, Truth, Forgiveness. On one occasion the quality is something tangible. What Gendler writes about it serves as a brief introduction to the book: "The Wind is a wonderful storyteller. I still remember how she introduced me to the Qualities when I was a child" (Gendler 1984, first piece, unpaged).

In a submerged first-person point of view, Gendler writes a minisketch about each quality, calling it by name, personifying it, describing its actions, thoughts, desires, history, and habits. Every now and then, she has the quality she is writing about interact with another quality (Trust is the daughter of Truth. Competition loves Creativity but marries Efficiency. Anxiety's friends are Worry, Terror, Doubt, and Panic). These miniatures are often brief, between fifty and one hundred words, though sometimes they extend to several hundred, only rarely, however, running over a page in length. Thirty-four of the qualities are enhanced with Gendler's whimsical line drawings.

I wanted students to know about quality writing as a possibility for their multigenre papers. I decided to try the exercise myself—teacher-as-writer, you know, practice what you preach, experience yourself what you are about to ask students to do. Here is a sixth draft of my quality experiment:

Regret

(After The Book of Qualities *by J. Ruth Gendler)*

Regret sits on the edge of my bed at midnight, jabbing me in the ribs. "You blew that lesson," says Regret. "You weren't clear . . . didn't model what you wanted . . . didn't grade fairly . . . were too demanding . . . too lenient . . . didn't give students enough time." Regret never forgets what went awry, fell short, fizzled. Regret not only sees the glass half empty, Regret sees what remains draining fast.

Regret resurrects particular students from decades ago. "How about Mary Ann Bennett your first year teaching?" says Regret. "She couldn't read or write. You just thought she was lazy. She quit school second semester. Remember when she came by to drop off her book and thanked you for being such a great teacher? Boy, if she thought that, she did need more education!"

At Happy Hour, Regret often meets with Success. They sit huddled in a corner and talk for hours. Regret blathers, harps, complains. Success listens, takes notes, makes plans. Regret and Success always share a cab home. Success always pays the fare.

I tried the quality writing exercise with my methods students, who had just returned from their first field experience. Without telling them what I was up to, I had them brainstorm emotions, feelings, issues, and abstractions they associated with ten consecutive mornings spent working in high school English classrooms. I showed them "Regret," the emotion I felt in my teaching more often than I liked to admit. Next, I introduced them to *The Book of Qualities*, showed them three of Gendler's sketches. We made explicit what Gendler had done in order to write them:

- Make the quality a character. Call it by name.
- Use third-person point of view or submerged first person.
- Say things directly about the quality. This is "direct characterization." The writer supplies indisputable facts—"Regret never forgets what went awry." "Despair has a heart condition." "Confidence is humble."
- Have the quality act. This is "indirect characterization." Readers infer character traits from what the quality does and says. Instead of saying, for example, that Regret is insistent, nagging, and bothersome, I describe Regret sitting on the edge of my bed at midnight, "jabbing me in the ribs."
- Let the quality interact with another quality if that will add a complication or payoff, like Regret and Success meeting at Happy Hour.

We all chose a quality from the list we'd made and spent ten minutes freewriting à la Gendler. Then we shared some, the creative current spreading throughout the classroom. I asked students to type their drafts and to tinker with them if they had an urge to say more or less or something else. And, of course, if they were so moved, they could write a new one. Here's Alaina writing about a quality most of the students had felt:

Exhaustion

Exhaustion rolls out of bed in the morning (after hitting the snooze button several times, of course). She grudgingly drags herself into the shower, staring blankly at the wall as hot water rains down on her. Exhaustion is always running late. She grabs her book bag and dashes out the door, forced to run all the way to her first class, only to realize that she grabbed the wrong notebook. She stumbles numbly through the day, always on the brink of nodding off, never managing to shake the lethargy from her bones.

When midnight rolls around, Exhaustion is wide awake. She frequently meets up with her good friend, Procrastination, for dinner, which then, of course, turns into an inevitable four-hour event. It's 2 AM, and Exhaustion is *still* awake, typing furiously on her laptop, trying to finish that paper she really should have started on Monday. Finally, at 5AM, Exhaustion calls it a night. She falls into bed and is asleep within seconds. Her alarm rings shrilly three hours later, the harshest of all wake-up calls. Exhaustion stumbles blearily out of bed, ready to start the cycle over again.

Alaina Conti, college junior

Quality pieces have become a staple in my students' multigenre papers. I don't require them, but many students see the possibilities. Aaron, a mechanical engineering major, was enamored with freewriting. He had quickened to the idea of using language to craft his written voice and explore the landscape of his mind. In his multigenre paper he traced the history of freewriting, described the nineteenth century psychological origins of stream of consciousness, and showed how freewriting might work in teaching people to write. He included this quality piece:

Freewriting

Freewriting is a good friend and a great listener. She often stops by whenever you need someone to help clear your head, or to kick-start the engine of the mind.

Freewriting works as a midwife. She also trains others in her profession. Her most accomplished student is Imagination. It was Imagination who was Freewriting's midwife when she gave birth to Art.

Freewriting's older twin, Writers-Block, could not be more different from her. He moves in when he is not invited, and stays until Freewriting forces him out.

Freewriting is always a pleasure to spend time with. Especially when she brings young Art with her.

Aaron Hudson, college freshman

John was a student in the teacher preparation program at Miami and also a midshipman in the Naval Reserve Officer Training Corps. He was upbeat, conscientious, possessed of an engaging sense of humor, and dedicated to joining the military. In his multigenre research of the Marine Corps, he realized that two qualities were inextricably bound:

History and Tradition

History loves Tradition but gets sick of Tradition following him around all the time. History is wise beyond his years and everyone always looks to him for answers. He constantly reminds people of what was and what is to come. Tradition, on the other hand, finds what he thinks are the best traits of History and mimics them—forever. Tradition is a wonderful thing, for he keeps History fresh in the minds of everyone lest his wonderful vault of knowledge be forgotten. Unfortunately, Tradition is loyal to History to a fault. "So what if your newfangled idea makes sense," Tradition says. "We've been doing it like this for two hundred years."

"That's exactly the point," Change pipes in. "The old way is more than outdated. This way is faster, cleaner, easier, and cheaper."

"I'll have none of it," Tradition replies.

History sits by quietly for he knows that Change is inevitable. He also knows that Tradition is nearly impossible to reason with.

John Casey, college junior

Rigor is a word much bandied about these days. With writing, most people associate rigor with argument, thesis, claim, evidence. Anything that smacks of creativity is soft, fluffy, cuddly, lax, decidedly unrigorous. I don't buy such thinking. And I will add this: my suspicion is that those who dismiss the rigor of creative writing have not done much creative writing themselves.

Writing quality pieces à la Gendler nudges students to analyze their topics, draw upon their personal experience and knowledge, synthesize their thinking while adding flesh and blood to abstractions. They use direct and indirect characterization, just as novelists do. They go beyond simply *recognizing* personification on a multiple-choice test to actually *applying* what they know by personifying something. They consider comparisons and contrasts as they think about introducing other qualities into their sketches. They work with implication and inference.

They write incisively. And writing in present tense lets them experience the immediacy and urgency of that underused verb tense. Writing in the style of Ruth Gendler is also fun, which does not preclude rigor.

For me, writing sometimes continues after I have printed what I think is a final copy. A year after I finished writing that sixth draft, I had occasion to reread "Regret." I read as a stranger to my own words, which enabled me to notice what I had not noticed when I was immersed in them. Something did not hold true in that final paragraph that I had been so proud of—Regret and Success meeting at Happy Hour. That wasn't right. That wasn't true to my own craft as a teacher. I revised one more time:

> At Happy Hour, Regret often meets with Reflection. They sit huddled in a corner and talk for hours. Regret blathers, harps, complains. Reflection listens, takes notes, makes plans. Regret and Reflection always share a cab home. Regret pays the fare, for he knows that tomorrow he'll meet with Success.

That revision accurately describes my teaching. And the word work was fulfilling, as I crafted the sketch to surprise the reader by placing the payoff in the last word of the last sentence. I'm respectful of how moving away from my writing for a time lets me look at it as a stranger. I'm no longer married to my creation, feel free, in fact, to tinker with the language, change meaning, get closer to truth. I once heard the poet Billy Collins say, "Students think revision is cleaning up after the party. They have it wrong. Revision *is* the party." I concur. Revision is the part of writing that's most rewarding. For me, it's fun and venturesome. Most of my busy college students are not convinced of this. They see revision as a chore, something that slows down getting their papers finished. Being "a one and done writer" is their preferred writing process. Once in awhile my persistent teaching of revision yields a change in attitude: "Revision can open new doors and close old ones," writes Tracy Gray. "It can clean house and make room for new ideas." And Jackie notes how she amended her misconception about the work of writing: "Even published authors struggle with their own writing, which I usually don't imagine because sometimes I get sucked into the idea that authors are experts without drafts."

I'll plug away, teaching students how they might revise their writing, showing them the movement I make in my own drafts. Some semester I fully expect a student to catch me after class and say, "Dr. Romano, this final draft isn't quite what I want. I need to get some distance, then revise. I'll get back to you in a year."

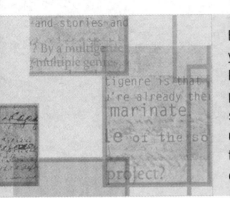

Buy *The Book of Qualities* and enjoy. Share Gendler's style with your students. Examine qualities found in literature: Ma Joad's Perseverance, Courage, Integrity, capacity for Love. Holden's penchant for Prevarication, his Cynicism, his Obsession to save Innocence. Have your students Gendlerize them. And naturally then, lead students to tease out qualities and themes of their multigenre research and use that as material to produce quality writing.

"[T]he prose horse is in harness, a good, sturdy and comfortable harness, while the horse of poetry has wings. And I would rather fly than plow."

Mary Oliver, poet, *Long Life: Essays and Other Writings*

"I was convinced writing poems would be the death of me, yet here I am."

Dana Buchholz, graduate student

When my sister's husband of twenty years was dying of cancer, she sent me a poem she wrote:

Near The End

Tommy sleeps more hours each day.
He woke at 11:00 tonight.
I gave him his meds and rubbed
his back with baby powder.
He said, "How long do I have to stay here?"
"Well, Tom," I said, "whenever you are feeling
better and want to leave, it's OK."
He said, "But how long do you want me to stay?"
I said, "Tommy, you know how much I love you,
but I've taken care of everything now.
Whenever you want to leave, it's fine."
He said, "Sounds like a winner to me."
I asked if anyone had come after him yet
and he said, "No, not yet."
And now he has fallen back into a deep sleep.

My sister didn't know she'd written a poem. She simply focused on describing this moment from the last days she and her husband were spending together. Nancy's original writing to me began like this:

```
From: _____@aol.com
Date: Wed, 18 Oct 2006 00:09:10 EDT
Subject: just me
To: romanots@muohio.edu
X-Real-ConnectIP: 64.12.137.7
```

As so often happens when my students write about tough sub-jects—as I am reading about the slaughter they have come through—I think, "What great writing." That's what I felt as I read my sister's email. In unpretentious language produced out of weariness and love, she honored the time of Tommy's passing. She wrote a poem and didn't know it. I merely cut one *some* and three *ands*, rearranged four words, inserted line breaks, and titled it. The poem emerged because my sister sought to be direct and specific, reporting the imagery, the facts, and the dialog of this indelible moment with her husband of two decades. In doing so she created a mood of peace, quietude, and acceptance that played out in the living room of their apartment. I felt privileged she had used language to let me be present.

Students often arrive in my classes with inflated notions of poetry, what it is, where it comes from, what you have to do to write it. In her last semester of college, one student wrote this as part of a self-assessment of her learning:

> Sometimes I get so caught up in metaphor that I forget what I'm writing about. This especially trips me up in poetry when I thought the whole point was lofty metaphor. I'm still reeling over your assertion in class a few weeks ago, Dr. Romano, when we read poetry by Ken Brewer. You applauded his clarity and accessibility. Poetry is supposed to do that?!?
>
> *Jessi Roesch, college senior*

I confess that I do like poetry best when it's clear and accessible, which doesn't always mean that one reading gives me a satisfying experience. Sometimes after reading a poem I just feel something I can't articulate. I must reread to deepen the meaning. Poetry, I want my students to see, doesn't have to be a puzzle. It doesn't have to be obscure, ambiguous, impenetrable, despite our experience reading poems that overmatched us when we were students.

Since 1988, in each class I teach, before attendance, announcements, or any activity, I read aloud a poem, or rather, I orally interpret a poem. I bring to my reading all I know about language, writing, and the expressive possibilities of voice. I pay respect to each word. The poem I read is usually contemporary and usually free verse. We don't analyze it or look for hidden meanings. We don't deconstruct its pattern of imagery.

My purpose is to get the great language of our best writers into people's bones. Those fresh observations, keen perceptions, surprising metaphors, vivid descriptions, those final lines that often bring imagery and meaning together asudden. Such poems leave alert readers moved. I read poems by Marge Piercy, Mary Oliver, Billy Collins, MeKeel McBride, Barbara Crooker, Raymond Carver, Stanley Kunitz, and many lesser known poets, sometimes even former students . . . the roster is long and ever growing. I have old favorites, of course, but I also browse the poetry shelves in good bookstores. Electronically, I receive Ted Kooser's "American Life in Poetry" each week and Garrison Keillor's "The Writer's Almanac" each morning. Kooser and Keillor introduce me to many new poems. Sometimes I like a poem and the author's voice so much that I order the book the poem is printed in. To keep track of all these memorable poems, I've accumulated twelve three-ring binders, each containing poems in categories I've devised: poems about people, places, mortality, family, and teaching/learning; poems that affirm life; poems about holidays, sports, art, writing, reading, youth, and aging.

In her final learning portfolio one semester, a student—now a high school English teacher—wrote of her coming to poetry after hating it through high school and much of college:

> I didn't know there were live poets until college (okay, so I'm exaggerating a bit, but really!). Poets like Taylor Mali and Daniel Beatty changed my way of thinking. Poetry was honest, realistic, moving and inspiring. I could write poetry. I could create a flowing piece of art that was beautiful, to me, if not anyone else. I became immersed in everything Taylor Mali had to say and moved by even dead poets like Robert Frost.
>
> You, Dr. Romano, read me beautiful poems every class. Because of this I know I am a "yam of a woman." Because of poetry, I know where

my classmates are from and I know who needs forgiven. Even if I only read a poem every day to show my students how beautiful poems are, they will get more than I did. And I will do more than read; like Taylor Mali would say in spoken word, "I'll make them write, write, write, and I'll make them read." I want students to write poems. I want them to see the power in getting their thoughts on paper. Writing is power; writing poetry is beautiful power.

Brittany Blevins, college junior

But how to get students to write poems in their own true voices, not revert to sing-song patterns, forced rhymes, and lofty sentiments? How to get students to write poems with language that is direct, clear, vivid, accessible?

The prolific poet and wise teacher, William Stafford, once wrote that "a poem is a lucky piece of talk" (Stafford 1986, 58). When writing poems, our students should forget their notions of what a poem is. They should instead concentrate on language. Be direct and specific with the language in them as they report their perceptions in words. That's the way to stumble into language with a little luck in it. That's what my sister did in capturing her husband's voice, his anxiety, sense of humor, and relief. She saw the peace he had come to, and she caught it in words.

Description: See It, Say It, See It Further

If there is one thing I want to get through to students, it is this: Much of our best poetry is largely description—something perceived, rendered, and extended as the poet's actual saying drives her to see further. The description often uses figurative language, metaphors or similes that leave your mouth agape or head nodding, impressed, moved, startled. Maybe you reread not because you didn't understand but because you want to experience it again, the language is so precise and striking, so how-could-it-be-otherwise. And the poem is mostly pure description, like our bodies are mostly salt water.

One poet I am sure to introduce to my students is Marge Piercy, one of our enduring poetic voices of the past fifty years. In "The Woman in the Ordinary" (1973), Piercy describes women as they appeared in advertisements and consumer products of mid-twentieth century America, images demure, sainted, hallowed, worthy of placing on a pedestal . . . and then dismissing. In opposition to this, Piercy describes another woman who waits inside, complex, vital, outspoken, ready to break free: "a yam of a woman of butter and brass" (Piercy 1973, 32). Pure description, metaphorical, sensory, connotative, the oppression of the past and the potential locked within both unmistakable.

In "The Summer Day" Mary Oliver wonders at the simple marvels of the world as she strolls through fields. The poem is nineteen lines long; Oliver spends eight of those lines describing in intricate detail the movements and look of a grasshopper that has lighted on her hand. In the last nine lines, she describes the idle way she has spent the day, observing the natural world, praying, really, in her own observant, appreciative, meditative way. In the final two lines of the poem, she turns from description and explanation to confront readers directly with a question: How do they intend to live their "one wild and precious" lives (Oliver 1992, 94). It's one of the most philosophically profound endings I've ever read, a simple inquiry with two perfect adjectives. Long ago when I read "The Summer Day" to a group of student teachers I was supervising, one of them—when I finished that final line—burst into tears.

In his reverent poem, "At the Cancer Clinic," one of our past poet laureates, Ted Kooser, describes a frail woman, wearing a knitted cap, being helped by her two sisters to walk through the waiting room, their goal, the smiling, encouraging nurse waiting in an open doorway, "How patient she is in the crisp white sails/of her clothes." The sisters' progress is slow and careful. The final line shifts our attention from the sisters and nurse to something else: "all the shuffling magazines grow still" (Kooser 2004, 7). Through pure description, we know we have witnessed courage, love, and grace.

If I could just get my students to slow down and describe well the focus of their attention, if I could get them to forget rhyme, forget allegiance to a tight form, forget some set rhythm. . . . Just describe, so readers (and they themselves) experience what they are writing about. That would be enough, even though I realize there is much more to writing poems than description. There is the length of the lines, how those lines end—often with a strong word, the rhythm of the words the poet puts together, the white space between stanzas, the economy of language, the compression of meaning. There are books we can read that will deepen our understanding of writing poems. We can turn what we learn into minilessons to help our students write well.

In an article about teaching high school students to write poems, Maureen Barbieri says that all poetry, whether Geoffrey Chaucer or Taylor Mali, "is about sound and about surprise" (Barbieri 2007, 115). That's why I read poems aloud to my students. That's why I sometimes even read aloud poems when I'm alone. In poems we find not only some of the best language, but also some of the best arrangement of that language. The very sound of saying it is pleasurable. And surprise? That's the poet's perception. That's Piercy's "yam of a woman," Oliver's grasshopper as you've never seen one before, and Kooser's nurse in the "crisp white sails of her clothes."

A Poem and the Poet's Commentary

I came to know Ken Brewer when I taught at Utah State University from 1991 to 1995. Ken wrote poetry, taught poetry, and headed the graduate program in English. When Ken was diagnosed with pancreatic cancer in 2005, he was Utah's poet laureate and at the height of his skills as a poet. He was clear-eyed, tough-minded, and compassionate. Through most of the nine months of his illness, he wrote poetry about what was happening to him. "I'm a poet," he said in a CBS interview, "This is what I do." In the introduction to his posthumously published *Whale Song: A Poet's Journey into Cancer*, he wrote, "Writing began to heal my spirit" (Brewer 2007, Foreword unpaged). His writing was a balm to my spirit, too, as I waited to lose a friend of fifteen years.

Here is a poem Ken sent to me three months after the diagnosis:

Waiting for the Dog

Gus is a black miniature schnauzer
with a red collar. When we let him out
at night in our fenced-in back yard,
still we put a plastic collar on him.

It blinks a pink light so we can see
that he hasn't vanished in the dark.

I understand this need for coming home,
for being safe in the house, as in place
as the couch, the table, the kitchen sink.
Perhaps, I, too, need a collar with lights
to keep me ashore, to let everyone know
that I am here no matter how dark the night.

Pure description of simple, tangible things: schnauzer, night, fenced-in yard, blinking light. Ken describes what he notices, and he doesn't let go of his description but uses it to imagine, explore, and speculate. Since I knew Ken, the poem carries extra emotional impact for me. But as I said before, the teacher in me also notices the writing craft. In this case, I wondered, too, about making the poem. I wrote to Ken, asking him about the creation of "Waiting for the Dog." In an email message, Ken described his writing process:

> Tom—I never know where a poem is heading as I begin it. After writing "Waiting for the Dog," I began to think of the title as a subtle hint of "Waiting for Godot" and the metaphor in the second stanza surprised me too. That shift from a light in a dark back yard to a light in a light tower along some coast, bringing in the sea/water image (or symbol). That just came as I was writing, with no plan at all. It's a leap, but I think it works and I don't mind "leaps." I prefer to start a poem with something that gives me image and detail (foundation) right away, then write to expand that to some other level or meaning. Always, the language surprises and teaches me.

Start with images and details; follow where they lead. Trust what's been noticed. No plan but to describe. Be comfortable with not knowing where the poem is headed. Welcome surprises of language and meaning. There is a sense of adventure in Ken's attitude, a willingness, a longing even, to discover and encounter the unexpected. I'd like to see Ken's credo written into a Common Core standard for learning to write: "Students will learn to write expansively, trusting language to lead them to surprises of meaning and insight."

The key here, I think, is *language*. Too often in writing anything, our attention is taken by form or audience or propriety. We forget about language, using it in good faith, trusting its powers of discovery. Actually creating words on the page leads to meaning, connections, associations, ideas, and refinements of ideas—things we did not have until we engaged in the process of writing. Language is our canoe up the wilderness river, our bush plane, our space capsule, our magic. Instead of "now you see it, now you don't," using language works in reverse: "now you don't see it, now you do."

Pure description will carry students a long way in writing poems. That and work, of course, fooling with the words, trying and testing and considering alternatives, moving from first blurt to discovery to crafting language, whether we are seventh graders or Pulitzer Prize winners.

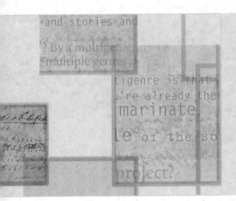

Surround your students with poems, the kinds of poems you want them to write. Read them silently. Read them aloud. Give them voice. Read with a clarity and deliberate speed that respect the words. Talk about how the poems work. Ask students to jot their perceptions of their topic. What have they noticed from their inside knowledge? From their research? What things are similar? Pick out one perception and describe it with detail, without judgment. Like Ken Brewer, follow language where it leads.

Student Poem That Sucks

I'll leave you with a poem written by a "strategic communication" major, who rediscovered the pleasures of writing poetry her senior year of college. Suzanne researched the legends, history, mythology, and pop culture of vampires. You'll understand why I thought that Suzanne had been enrolled in one of Miami University's most popular courses: Botany 224 "The Vitriculture and Enology of Wine" (grape growing and wine making). Read first what Suzanne had to say about writing the poem:

> I worked on this poem (a lot) until I got my voice to sound just as I wanted
> it. It's written from the perspective of a vampire, and I wanted to approach

the subject as tongue-in-cheek. Vampires in fiction today are represented as either terrifying and gruesome or as playful and seductive. Here, I used my voice to find the humor in vampires.

This piece is primarily description. I worked to use adjectives that come alive and breathe. I wanted to convey the speaker's passion for blood, the way some people are passionate about wine. I liked the opportunity to play with words here (for example, "like a penny, if you were to suck off the shine"). I love to work with words and pull at the senses.

I also make a point to emphasize diction in my writing. Phrases like "plump black cherries" jump out at the reader and add inflection. I chose a lot of my words during the revision phase, when I really wanted my words to pack a punch.

taste.

warm and thick
it pulsates from the vein
moving
    streaming
       living.
a favorite, you ask?
well I like it all, but i suppose it depends on the day.

o negative.   fresh.
sharp, crisp.
a bit like a penny, if you were to suck off the shine.
a hint of acai berry.

b positive. oh, b positive.
more rich, more dense, more . . . decadent.
iron, bold but graceful. deep.
minor undertone of grapes, the red variety.
    juicy.

a positive.
the chicken of vital fluids.
common, perhaps dull, but versatile.
distinct aroma of plump black cherries,
rounded out by smooth tannins.

but ah, ab negative.
a delicacy.
the escargot, if you will. the caviar.
spicy, earth-scented.
smooth, silky to the
                              finish.

Suzanne Evans, college senior

ONE WAY TO LAUNCH STUDENTS INTO POETIC IMAGININGS IS to have them imitate the approach of someone else's poem. I'm talking about more here than, say, writing in a particular form, like sonnets, haiku, or villanelles, though doing that, too, is worthwhile. Here I'm talking about using poems as mentor texts in approach, language, and maybe even in subject matter. Such imitation has a long, respected tradition among poets. The technique is called "copy-change," which requires students to imitate an experienced poet's poem and then "thank" that poet for what they have learned about how "to structure poems, end lines, and work with specific images" (Dunning and Stafford 1992, 91). The thanking usually comes after the title when students credit their poetic inspiration by writing, for example, "In the style of Mekeel McBride" or "After McBride's 'The Truth About Why I Love Potatoes.'"

When my wife and I flew back from Utah where we had visited our friend, Ken Brewer, just two days before his death, I needed to write beyond the pages of my notebook. I knew I had seen Ken for the last time. I had spent three hours at his bedside. I had touched him, told him how much better my life had been for having him in it. I'd said goodbye. A William Stafford poem provided me with a way to say more (1993, 55):

Report to Ken Brewer, Poet Laureate of Utah
(After Stafford's "Report To Crazy Horse")

Your email update two weeks before you died kept me awake.
Covers tucked under my chin could not warm me.
Cancer had narrowed your life to the bed. You spoke in whispers,
had little energy left to document your dying, as you'd done
for nine months in poems swift, sure, alive.

I don't like losing friends, Ken. No more poems from Brewer
is a future bereft. After diagnosis you healed your spirit with pen
    and paper

in that place you lived forty years, where language let you explore,
critique, and celebrate, especially the tough stuff.

For nine months you wrote about it all: pine siskins squabbling
at the bird feeder, radiation, visits from friends at twilight,
   chemotherapy,
the black fur of Gus—the schnauzer, the mountains circling Cache
   Valley hugging you
all and Bobbie, your wife, bringing zinnias: red, pink, and orange.

The memory of your fierce heart drives me to be a better man.
The day before you died, March still wintry here in southern Ohio,
I pressed seeds into soil in the greenhouse.
For days I watered, monitored temperature, stayed patient.

Early spring is possibility. Though some seeds never germinate,
most push through soil and reach for sun.
In May I'll transplant tomato, pepper, eggplant, basil.
I'll compost, water, weed. Months from now, harvest will come.

You were not a gardener, Ken. You were teacher, poet, friend.
Yet you knew how to sow, how to nurture growth, stay steadfast.
Next spring, seeds from this year's garden will quicken.
You journeyed from that Indiana boyhood to poet laureate,
to a man so many counted as friend.
You knew that possibility is enough start for anyone.

That poem was good for me to write then. And it is good for me
to tinker with and revise as I write *Fearless Writing*. It was my urge,
my need, seven years ago to speak to Ken, to gather some of what
he was like, to write beyond his death and the grief I was feeling,
to name what I appreciated about him. After my visit to Ken, why
did Stafford's "Report to Crazy Horse" bubble up, unbidden, in my
consciousness? Why that poem? I'd admired the Sioux leader since
childhood. Through my reading as an adult, I'd learned that Crazy
Horse, *Tasunka Witko* in Lakota (Power 2010, 7), was courageous
and compassionate, tender and fierce, a leader by example, independent of mind, great of spirit. Those were qualities I saw in Ken (plus
a sense of ironic humor, usually gentle, sometimes biting, that I'm not

sure Crazy Horse had). For whatever reason, I'm glad Stafford's poem had tucked itself away in me.

Imitating—copy changing—the style of a published poet, is a clear illustration of Vygotsky's "zone of proximal development." The student apprentices herself to a more experienced, more accomplished other. That happens in classrooms with a peer or a teacher. In this case, however, the accomplished other is a "distant teacher" (John-Steiner 1985). In imitating the style of a poem, students stretch themselves, try something they wouldn't on their own, perform beyond their present skill and development, changing and growing as a user of language, becoming more sophisticated in their understanding and practice of poetry.

One of the most imitated poems in the land over the last twenty years is George Ella Lyon's "Where I'm From" (1999). Track it down if you don't know it. The poem is upbeat, moving, accessible, perfect for imitating in form and content. I use it in the first week of my methods class to get students to write about something they know, to examine their roots and values with specific detail, imagery, parallel language structures, and understatement, just as Lyon does. When students wrote multigenre papers about a book they loved, Gina chose Khaled Hosseini's *The Kite Runner* (2003). Here is a poem she wrote revealing some of Afghanistan's culture and history and details of the narrator's life:

Where I'm From
(after George Ella Lyon)

I am from Afghanistan,
From Babalu the Boogeyman.
I am from a mother I killed.
I am from Islam.
From where drinking is a sin.
I am from Panjpar, where kings get killed,
And a *kursi* heats my legs.
I am from books and jokes,
From Persian heroes and walks through short cuts.
I am from naan covered with marmalade.
I am from where kites fall to the ground,

From a tree with mulberries.
I am from riches and parties.
From a place lacking televisions.
From a place devastated by Soviets.
I'm from where blameless people are shot and killed.

Gina Castelli, college junior

Opportunities for copy-change are endless. When you read poetry, read not just for enjoyment, but also with an eye for finding possibilities for imitation. Here are poems I've seen imitated:

"How to Live" by Charles Harper Webb

"She Just Wants" by Beverly Rollwagen

"Introduction to Poetry" by Billy Collins

"This is Just to Say" and "The Red Wheelbarrow" by William Carlos Williams

"Creed" by Meg Kearney

"In My Next Life" by Mark Perlberg

"Among the Things He Does Not Deserve" by Dan Albergotti

"Things I Know" by Joyce Sutphen

"My House" by Nikki Giovanni

"Jazz Fantasia," "Chicago," and "Prayers of Steel" by Carl Sandberg

The Truth About Why I Love UNH

One of the many delights that have accrued from my association over the past thirty years with the University of New Hampshire and the New Hampshire Summer Literacy Institutes is my friendship with irreplaceable people: Tom Newkirk, Linda Rief, Maureen Barbieri, Don Murray, Penny Kittle, Don Graves, Jane Hansen, many more. Another is the poet and teacher, Mekeel McBride. Since the first time I heard her read her poems, I've bought every book she's written. In *Dog Star Delicatessen* (2006, 51) is this poem that takes me beyond its subject matter. I remember in college my writing teacher calling such literature "deceptively simple."

The Truth About Why I Love Potatoes
for Sarah Apt

1.

Of everything you get for dinner
they're the most fun to play with:
gravy lakes soaking deep into the soft white Alps
of the mashed ones; French fries good for fences
to keep your fork safe from Lima beans;
the baked ones perfect for pounding down
into pancakes from the moon.

2.

I guess I forgot to mention how much I used to love
globbing mashed potato into a ball then hurling it
at my brother so it seemed he was the one
who had made the mess. Now I know grownups
do the same thing, too, but usually not with potatoes.

3.

If a potato were able to turn into a person,
I'm almost certain it would be someone you'd like
for a friend. It could teach you to understand
the language of animals who live underground:
worms and woodchucks, foxes and bears.
On rainy Saturday afternoons, it would take you
to funny movies. When you were feeling sad,
it would remind you of the good things
you'd forgotten about yourself.

4.

There might be dozens, even more, in the garden,
without you ever knowing, fat moons blooming
a secret night sky right under your feet.

5.

If I could have my wish, I'd want my poem
to be just like a potato. Not afraid of the dark.
Simple and surprising at the same time.

You'd have to dig a little to get it but then
you'd be glad you made the effort. And maybe
after you were finished, something in you
that had been hungry for a long time
wouldn't feel so empty anymore.

Just about every time I teach multigenre, I offer McBride's poem as a copy-change opportunity. Sometimes students' versions of it will show up in their papers, sometimes not, and sometimes the exploration leads to other writing. One notable time it appeared was when Leah wrote about the genocide in Rwanda in 1994. In a self-assessment of her work, Leah has this to say:

"The Truth About Why I Dig" is hands down the best piece in this paper. Maybe it was because I had the opportunity to focus on one particular story (most of the time I was overwhelmed by all the research and couldn't find a way to narrow it down) and devote a large chunk of time to it. It took me forever to write as well. It was challenging and required a lot of analysis and synthesis. I love the format (thank you, Mekeel McBride)—5-part segmentation and how each part has its own little thing going on. I took some liberties with Clea Koff's book, *The Bone Woman* (2004), but I think the resulting piece paints an incredible picture of the "after," and I think Clea would agree that it was worth it. It's risky, it's honest and it tells another side of the Rwandan story.

The Truth About Why I Dig
After Mekeel McBride. For Clea Koff, forensic anthropologist

1.
Of everything I dig up from the earth's unforgotten soil
It is the human skeleton that tells me the most:
Age, sex, stature, cause of death, and maybe even
Who these people were.

2.
I guess I forgot to mention that, as a little girl,
I used to love to collect the bodies

of dead birds
and bury them only so I could later dig them up.
But in the graves of the Kibuye church,
the people who committed these crimes
never thought that anybody would ever
dig up the bodies.

3.

As you dig, it's interesting how you immediately
look for points of comparison between
your own body and the body in front of you.
The bones can talk. They not only teach you
the language of the dead (a lesson of maggots and mummification)
but remind you of all the things you'd forgotten about yourself.

4.

In the clandestine graves, my bloodied knees and blistered
    fingertips
surface what remains of victim after victim
with the hope that I can find the heads
and reunite them with their bodies. I take the "after" and
deduce the "before" in quest of naming the nameless and
revealing how they were killed. I want to
return them to their families and prove to the UN
that these were not combatants.

5.

I don't dig to uncover those who had once been
buried "properly." I don't dig so that I can one day
brag to a lecture hall of eager undergraduates
about the time I ran out of flags that mark
human remains scattered on the hillside in Kigali.
But rather, I dig because
within the dead bodies there are living stories
waiting . . .
    . . . to be unearthed.

Leah Wessman, college senior

As a teacher I am always inviting, encouraging, pushing. If students heed my urging, they will, I believe, surprise themselves with accomplishment, satisfy a hunger in them, be reminded of good things they had forgotten about themselves, like what they were capable of when they wrote with good faith. When I discover that students are pushing themselves, that's even better. A double major in creative writing and English Education, Liz found a poem to imitate in "Unit of Measure" by Sandra Beasley (2009). The first line is "All can be measured by the standard of the capybara." In her copy-change Liz wrote about an animal she had loved since childhood, the wondrous orange beast of symmetry and the burning bright. Liz knew things, but you'll guess some of the detail she learned through research and was able to pack into her poem:

Unit of Measure (after Sandra Beasley)

All can be measured by the standard of the tiger.
Everyone is lesser than or greater than the tiger.
Everything is taller or shorter than the tiger.
Everything is a mascot for a sugary breakfast cereal
more or less frequently than the tiger.
Everyone eats greater or fewer antelope
than the tiger. Everyone eats more or less birds.
Everyone mews more or less than the tiger,
who also growls, roars, grunts, but unlike your house cat,
is unable to purr. Everyone is more or less able to purr
than a tiger, who—because his species
is quickly going extinct—might not have many reasons to purr.
Everyone is more or less a carnivore
than the tiger. Or going by the scientific name,
more or less *Panthera tigris*.
Everyone is used in tribal medicine
more or less often than the tiger, who,
because of rich mythological history,
is killed for medicinal purposes everyday.
Everyone is used as a rug more or less than the tiger.
Before you decide that you are

greater than or lesser than a tiger, consider,
that while your skin is one uniform color,
the tiger's skin, like his trademark stripes,
is just as striped.
Consider if you have had stripes.
Consider that while the tiger has
fewer teeth than most carnivores—only 32—
it has far more deadly teeth than you.
Consider how the tiger prefers to swim
with its head above the water.
Accept that you can swim better than a tiger.
Accept that you can walk among the prey of a tiger,
and not disturb them. *Safe*, they whisper to you, *you are safe.*

Liz Henderson, college junior

Give students an opportunity to ease into their own poems through a copy-change activity. You'll get better results if you discuss with students the features of a particular poem, like Mekeel McBride's "The Truth About Why I Love Potatoes," and then join them in 10–15 minutes of focused writing in which they try their own version. The idea is not that students must use this poetic experiment in their multigenre paper, but that they launch language doing their own exploring of a road that has been traveled before them. Students will generate words, images, and ideas they can fool with, as Leah says she did—that's always a good thing. Maybe trying this activity once will open the door to students finding their own favorite poems to copy-change.

CHAPTER 21

Prose Poetry

WHAT OF PROSE POEMS? ISN'T THAT AN OXYMORON?

Poetry is poetry, and prose is . . . well . . . columns, essays, reports, fiction, radio commentaries, letters to the editor, master's theses, office memos, dissertations, legal briefs, biographical sketches, hard news stories, reviews, and more. Yet sometimes we read prose and sense something more compressed about the language, more sensory, something especially rhythmic, lyrical, almost incantatory.

We might call that a prose poem, a potent hybrid of writing that provides the comfort of prose with the compression of poetry. Below is the great poet Mary Oliver offering a definition of prose poems:

> What you see on the page is a fairly short block of type—a paragraph or two, rarely more than a page. It looks like prose. Perhaps it has characters, perhaps not. Often, it is pure description. It usually does have the same sense of difference from worldly or sequential time that one feels in a poem. And it does certainly ask to be read with the same concentration, and allowance for the fanciful and the experimental, that we give to the poem.
>
> Because the prose poem is brief . . . it seems more often than not to have at its center a situation rather than a narrative. Nothing much happens, that is, except this: through particularly fresh and intense writing, something happens to the reader—one's felt response to the "situation" of the prose poem grows fresh and intense also.
>
> What is especially fascinating about prose poems is the problem of making the language work without the musicality of the line. The syntax found in prose poems is often particularly exquisite, combining power and grace. (1994, 86–87)

Prose poem is a sweetly slippery concept. Oliver says it might even have characters. Given their brevity then, prose poems could be confused with flashes. There is room in prose poems for the "fanciful" and "experimental." I like that. A situation, not so much a narrative, not so much plot with a character who yearns and someone or something blocking that yearning.

In matters of writing, I often default to Whitman, who wrote in many genres over his lifetime: an early novel, newspaper reports, reviews, traditional nineteenth-century rhymed poetry, political nonfiction, and, of course, barrier-breaking free verse. The following excerpt from the preface of *Leaves of Grass* stands as one of America's early prose poems:

> Love the earth and sun and the animals, despise riches, give alms to everyone that asks, stand up for the stupid and crazy, devote your income and labor to others, hate tyrants, argue not concerning God, have patience and indulgence toward the people, take off your hat to nothing known or unknown or to any man or number of men, go freely with powerful uneducated persons and with the young and with the mothers of families, read these leaves in the open air every season of every year of your life, re-examine all you have been told at school or church or in any book, dismiss whatever insults your own soul, and your very flesh shall be a great poem. (n.d., xxviii)

In this prose poem we have a directive from one of our great poets about how to live: generously, openly, in harmony with others—all others—yet with a strong sense of self and integrity of mind. Live this way, Whitman says, weighing everything against your own values, and your very time on earth will be a poem, a great poem. To urge us to his way of thinking, Whitman employs sinewy verbs: love, despise, stand, devote, hate, argue, take, go, read, dismiss, shall be. The piece might not be pure description in the way we usually think of description with color, movement, and sensory appeal, but Whitman certainly goes beyond the worldly and isn't concerned with sequential time. This writing is for all time. And fanciful? Try this: A human life with potential to be a poem. Impossible. Yet I believe it. I've seen such poems of flesh and blood. You have, too.

One of my graduate students, immersed in studying literacy education and newly quickened to constructivist learning theory, wrote a prose poem in which she is led by verbs to assert beliefs she has synthesized:

Making Meaning

Open a book. Roll around in the language. Allow it to penetrate your soul. Cry tears when the characters cry. Wipe your blood when they bleed. Feel their pain. Pay attention to the details of the words. Become the rhythm. Become intoxicated by scenery and dialogue. Contemplate the ideas contained between the covers. Let them invade your soul. Find peace. Know love and anger, injustice and frustration. Channel it. Learn about its source. Look closely into the nature of what it means to be truly human. Dig deep. Then dig deeper. This is what it's like to be alive.

Jen Gajus, graduate student

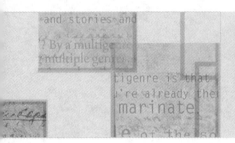

Do any characters in your multigenre topic have strong views about how to live or how to accomplish something? In light of your topic, do you, the author, have such strong views? Write a piece in the style of Whitman's prose poem, maybe in the way Jen wrote about reading with short, verbful sentences.

In Chapter 19 I made a case for poetry being driven by pure description, the writer perceiving, perhaps, only an indelible image, like a black schnauzer with a blinking pink light in a black back yard, then writing deeply with detail to see more clearly, taking readers along to see anew. Mary Oliver acknowledges the often pure descriptive nature of prose poems.

Karen Gooch, a graduate student in our literacy program, wrote a multigenre paper about an abiding love of hers since she was a little girl and sat in sturdy, wooden chairs, her feet not touching the floor: libraries, their history, their value, their changing uses through the years. Karen worked at Miami's King Library and had plenty of insider knowledge. In a prose poem peppered with figurative language, alliteration, and empathy she writes about a special situation that occurs once each semester in a college library:

Twice a year, the library bustles in a frenzy. An unnerving end to a time when blood pressures escalate, nerves unravel and the notion of a good night's sleep seems an empty promise. The doomsday of classes sweeps in, consuming thoughts. Finals week is in the air, a thick cloud of apprehension. Library overdrive, overflowing rooms, club-like claustrophobia, an air of burdening pressure. Study rooms battled over to the death. Swords unsheathed and battle cries warranted. Every man for himself in a predatory hunt for a nook not inhabited by gossiping girls or overstressed business majors. Study carrels secured heavily with lock and key. Remember to step lightly over corpselike bodies sprawled on floors. Spastic students, doped up on their roommate's Adderall, Red Bull, and Starbucks. Caffeine oozing through pores keeping bloodshot eyes open for one more word, one more line, one more paper.

Karen Gooch, graduate student

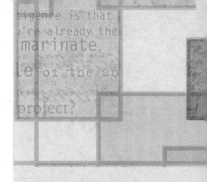

Another graduate student in a multigenre course I taught through Northeastern University on Martha's Vineyard one summer wrote about what it was like to teach high school in Alaska. Holly makes readers feel a central fact of her life during the school year. We felt it right there in a sweltering classroom on one of the great islands of the world:

Cold

You cannot breathe deep. The stab of cold won't let you. But you can smell it. You can hear it. You can taste it and feel it in the frozen marrow of your winter bones. You suck energy from the cold and use it to keep you warm. You must succumb and welcome it because it is two-faced and wants to be liked. Cilia and hair freeze and tinkle like shards of broken glass after a night of fighting and making up. The scarf wrapped around your thick face freezes solid. Your moisture, your life's water does not get far. It latches on and clings, full of life. Taste the salt sucked from your body. It is there on your scarf. You must drink more water in the cold than in the blazing equatorial sun. The frozen boundary sends heat back to your face and you know you are alive.

Step on it. Feel it. Hear it. Draw your energy from the cold. Step on the clean crisp snow—not fluffy white, but crusty and clumped. Kick it. Go ahead. This snow is kickable. Glass. It sounds like broken shards of glass after a night of fighting and making up.

The birds in the trees pack food around their brains to keep warm. They fluff their down and snuggle into each other, into the frozen world of fragile glass.

Holly Richardson, graduate student

Describe something central to your multigenre topic. Strive to write a prose poem by being purely descriptive, paying no attention to line length, allowing for the fanciful and experimental. Let the writing sit for two or three days. Come back to it as a friendly, word-wise stranger and hone the language, compress it and make it as fresh and intense as you can. See if you can achieve some of that power and grace of word order Mary Oliver says are part of prose poems.

22

Prose Poem or Flash Fiction— Which?

Trouble Sleeping

I am having trouble sleeping, so I know she is having trouble sleeping. You can't get that kind of news and not have trouble sleeping. Her mind always runs overtime, anyway. Whenever problems or worries come her way, she can forget about sleeping. She can forget about peace of mind even while she is at work in the hospital emergency room or cleaning the house or washing the dogs. There is no activity that empties her mind, except making love, maybe.

So when I am lying in bed wide awake, I know she is lying beside me wide awake, too.

"Why me?" she's thinking. "How did this happen to me?"

She has to be lying there thinking, because you know I am lying there thinking, "Why my wife? Why me? Why us?"

I'm in my own reverie lying there, sometimes self-pitying, sometimes angry and bitter and black, sometimes full of sorrow and compassion.

"Hold me," she says, "please hold me."

I do. I pull her against me and feel her breasts against my chest.

I WROTE THAT PIECE DURING THE MONTHS FOLLOWING MY wife's diagnosis of breast cancer in 1997. Through mastectomy, chemotherapy, breast reconstruction, yearly checkups with the oncologist, and a yearly mammography, we have been ever vigilant since. We don't live in fear of breast cancer returning or metastasizing, but we are aggressive in tracking down anything that might indicate trouble: a persistent, unrelenting headache, a white spot on a mammogram, a lump. We are not content with "It's probably nothing. We'll keep an eye on it." Knowing is almost always better than not knowing, and we want to know about cancer as soon as possible.

I wrote "Trouble Sleeping" to capture our experience the night after Kathy had had a lump removed, and we were waiting for biopsy results. I wasn't driven by genre. I was driven by our experience, by trying to render vividly what we were living, seeking to capture that complicated mix of fear, anxiety, bitterness, and love. In fact, I don't know if I could have articulated then in any expository way what we felt. We seemed so alone in the world that night. We had friends and family. We had daughter, Mariana. We had an excellent surgeon who was a family friend of twenty years. But what mattered that night, alone on our separate sides of the bed, was that we had each other. Words were important but only five were spoken. More importantly, we touched and held in that time of great need.

Is "Trouble Sleeping" a flash? It has characters. It certainly has yearning, the essence of a plot. It has dialog and paragraphs. It's the right length. Flash nonfiction, right? I'm not so sure. The piece has elements of prose poetry, too. There is music, a rhythm of sentences rocking back and forth, a repetition of key words, parallel language structures that are pleasurable to the ear amid the painful mystery that barely unfolds. This miniature snapshot reveals a situation, a moment of heightened emotion, just as much as it hints at plot. Is the syntax "particularly exquisite, combining power and grace"? You can decide that.

I introduce students to flash fiction and prose poems at the same time. First, I show them expository definitions of the two forms. Then we read Mary Oliver's "Blake Snake," a classic prose poem, ending with this memorable language as the black snake glides away: "his long body swaying like a suddenly visible song" (2002, 11). Then we read "The Paring Knife" by Michael Oppenheimer (1992), clearly a story with plot, character, movement, yearning, and a sweetly ambiguous ending. We talk and point to language that shows how the two examples conform to the expository definitions I've provided. We grow smug and sure with knowing the difference between flashes and prose poetry.

Then we examine pieces that blur boundaries between the two forms, as I think "Trouble Sleeping" does. Some of my students are exasperated by the closeness of the two subgenres. They want to know, definitively, which is which. In *Field Guide to Writing Flash Fiction*, writer and teacher Kim Chinquee writes, "all-in-all . . . [flash fiction and prose poetry] are simply interchangeable. Each can be the other" (Chinquee 2009, 113).

Prose poems and flashes exist on a continuum, prose poems being "more about language and poetics, whereas a flash carries more narrative and story" (Chinquee 2009, 112). The distinction between them is not worth quibbling about.

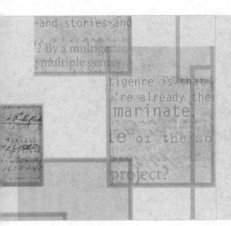

What situation is critical in your topic? What brief stories need told? Maybe you can't yet distinguish whether what is important is narrative with characters yearning or merely a situation that needs describing. All you feel is that what you notice seems important. Dive to the heart of it. Be specific in imagery and dialog. Remember Ken Brewer's openness to surprise, discovery, and leaps. You will, no doubt, write what you don't expect, maybe how to read well, the quality of cold, the jockeying in the library, the pain, pleasure, mystery, salvation, and redemption of love.

I LOVE ORDER AND ROUTINE. THEY HELP ME WRITE. THEY HELP me teach and cook and garden. But if I stayed only with the ordered and routine, my life would be the less. I'd never experience the other part of living: spontaneity, surprise, adaptation.

Three Clips of Welcoming the Unplanned and the Good Getting Better

Thirty years ago my lesson about Carl Sandberg's "Jazz Fantasia" is meticulously planned. I tell my high school juniors and seniors about jazz in the early part of the twentieth century. I tell them about poet-biographer-novelist-banjo player-folksong collector, much underrated American writer, Carl Sandberg, contemporary of Robert Frost and e. e. cummings. I orally interpret "Jazz Fantasia," getting the most out of the alliteration, metaphors, personification, and onomatopoeia. Students are silent, unmoved, maybe a little embarrassed for me, this teacher whose life is so empty he gets exercised about a poem on a Monday morning.

I'm exasperated, desperate, nearly sputtering: "If Sandberg had been writing now, he would *not* be writing about jazz"—and at that moment I'm struck by pedagogical lightning!—"he'd be writing 'Rock Fantasia,' 'Heavy Metal Fantasia,' 'Country Fantasia'—."

"Punk Fantasia?"

"You better believe it!" I say, roaring up to the challenge as I realize where this will go. "And that's your assignment: write your own poetic fantasy of the music you love." There's requisite moaning but most students perk up, despite themselves. This might be interesting. Later in the week, I collect the poems, sit on a stool in front of class, and although I'm reading cold, contending with all manner of handwriting, I give each poem a respectable, often rousing oral interpretation.

Says one student: "I didn't know I could sound so good!"

* * *

I take a snapshot of my May vegetable garden. Order prevails: rows of pepper plants, eggplants, tomato plants, each confined to sturdy steel cages from Gardeners Supply, planted in rows that are wide enough for me to till the soil. When the vines begin their sinewy journey, I'm beside those tomato plants almost every day, pinching suckers and training vines to grow inside the cages instead of out. By August the vines are riotous, spilling over the tops of the cages and stretching out on journeys I couldn't have predicted. I can barely make my way through the tilling path to harvest tomatoes. Squash, too—zucchini, Hybrid Zephyr, and butternut—have grown beyond their hills, covering peppers and eggplant, nudging the base of towering sunflowers. The August garden is a glorious jungle, my careful planning barely noticeable, control no longer possible. And the chaos yields bounty.

* * *

Kathy and I make many kinds of pasta sauce, but our basic sauce that carries us throughout the year is from my mother's recipe: chuck roast chopped into bite-sized pieces and browned in olive oil with oregano, salt, and pepper. To that she added tomato paste, tomato sauce, two whole garlic cloves, and, if she had it, a beef bone. To thin the mixture, she added two cups of water. The sauce simmered most of a day. It made supper that night and yielded several quarts for freezing.

Two years into our marriage, Kathy and I are suddenly struck: Why not use three times as much garlic and chop it into bits to spread out the pungent flavor? We do. In *The Godfather* we see Capo Clemenza make spaghetti sauce for the gangsters who had hit the mattresses in their war with the other Mafia families. He pours in red wine. Why, we wonder, are we adding water to thin the sauce? Why not dry red wine, like Uncle Gigi makes? We do, and the color of the sauce deepens red and the flavor of the sauce jumps. More than forty years now we've made our sauce that way.

* * *

Make room in your writing for the spontaneous, the accidental, the unplanned. One way to cultivate that room is to introduce students to "stream of consciousness," that mode of writing in which writers seek to communicate a character's mental experience—the language, sudden insights, diversions, images, emotions, rational thinking, sensations, memories—anything that might enter consciousness from both the psychological depths and the life happening around us. To capture stream of consciousness, the writer has to let go of control more than usual, trust the gush of language and associations even more. Oh, later we can shape and craft what ends up on the page, but the idea in the beginning is to write at the top of the lungs, so to speak, cutting loose a high speed voice of language and detail, capturing the illusion of thought in action.

Stephanie wrote a multigenre paper about her trip traveling in Europe the summer after her senior year of high school. At one point in a stream of consciousness, she dispenses with punctuation and capitalization to get closer to the actuality of thought, impressions, memories, prayer, and lingering anxiety about her travel companion:

on a bus in germany/switzerland in june
after high school graduation

first germany and then onto switzerland and the whole time I'm thinking God don't let her blow up don't let me make a wrong move or say something and if you could just please make it so that we both want to do the same thing at the same time and we can go hand-in-hand swallowed by the mouth of a great castle or antique shop or whatever she/me wants to do that day cause i can't take another scene like that in heidelberg and i really don't know why she got me so mad but when she blew her top i just wanted to put it back on her and say "here you boil for a bit because that's what i'm always doing" but she has the luxury of getting mad even if it's in the streets of a small german town over shoes and i look over and see her curled up across two seats on the bus her glasses are crooked on her face and i wonder who's going to understand her temper at college but I can't deal much longer cause i'm in europe for the first-maybe-last-time and every second is precious but i've been staring at the black forest countryside since heidelberg and i haven't seen a thing except her face reflected in the window

Stephanie Klare Adams, college sophomore

Show students Stephanie's example of stream of consciousness. Supplement that with examples from literature, if you like: William Faulkner, Virginia Wolf, a passage from Dalton Trumbo's *Johnny Got His Gun*. Talk about what the writer is doing with language and content to give the illusion of a mind in action. Get students to talk about how their minds work, what thought is actually like when it's running loose.

Set up a day for students to bring to class an idea from their topic: an emotional moment, one character's anxieties or yearnings, a bystander witnessing an event, a character speaking in a flood of love or anger or resolution, something that would lend itself to an unleashing of stream of consciousness. Invite students to break rules of grammar, punctuation, and usage if that helps them capture a river of conscious thought. Quickwrite for ten riotous minutes.

CHAPTER

24

**Where
the Mind
Wanders,
Part II**

Writing Dreams

"We need meaning, and dreams provide a nightly opportunity for it."

Kahla Davis, college junior, psychology major

DREAMS ARE DELICIOUS. NOWHERE ELSE IN MY LIFE DO I experience such vividness, mystery, anxiety, elation, and surreal madness. My daily, even life as a university professor electrifies during REM sleep, that time during slumber when my "skeletal muscles become so thoroughly relaxed they're virtually paralyzed" (Ackerman 2007, 160) and only the muscles of the eyes are not affected—my eyeballs "flit about wildly beneath" my lids (Ackerman 2007, 160–161), in those blessed, disconcerting rapid eye movements.

I heard an NPR talk-show guest once say, "We dream because the motor is running." When we dream,

> Silent are the regions of the prefrontal cortex known to be important in working memory, attention, and volition. The neurotransmitter systems required for these functions during waking . . . are simply shut off during REM sleep . . . with them go insight, reasoning, and logical sense of time. (Ackerman 2007, 161)

REM sleep "hosts the kind of delirious reverie characterized by strange, vivid hallucinations, illogical thinking, emotion, and confabulation" (Ackerman 2007, 161).

Not all the brain is quieted and at rest when we dream. Among active parts of the brain during REM sleep "are the amygdala and the limbic system, both central to the feelings of anger, anxiety, elation, and fear that so often accompany a dream story" (Ackerman 2007, 161).

Misfortune is a staple of dreams. Plans go awry. Chances are missed. People don't cooperate. Desires go unfulfilled. What happens is often bizarre. Our hauntings, anxieties, and fears show up in our dreams. Some months after my mother's death, for example, I dreamed of her standing with her fists on her hips, feet spread apart for stability, she so tiny and osteoporotic in the last years of her life. Mom looked off toward the horizon. Between us were dozens of shadowy figures, spread out randomly like pieces on a chessboard. I could see only her back. She saw something on the horizon I could not. No matter how I tried, I could not reach her side, could not wedge my way through the shadowy figures. I called her name, commanded her, "Mom, why are you dead?" Her gaze ahead did not waver. She never responded. It wasn't hard to interpret that dream and the grief and anxiety I felt from losing her after fifty years.

When I was nineteen, I got a summer job in a structural stoneware factory, where I spent eight hours a day facing another man, feet planted on wet pavement, pivoting my hips to the left to pick up a wire tray of three decorative pieces of stoneware and swinging then to my right to slide the tray into a large rack on wheels. When the rack was full, I pushed it aside while my workmate moved an empty rack into place. Then we worked double time, removing trays fast to catch up. Shutting down the line was verboten. That wasted time, slowed production, lost money. I came home that first day of work, dirty, feet wet, exhausted. I fell into bed fully clothed and awakened hours later when I dreamed of a relentless conveyer belt delivering tray upon tray I couldn't escape from. In junior high school I dreamed that an arrow—sharp point not quite touching the small of my back—chased me through the neighborhood, up and down staircases, through rooms, over stretches of field, all the while buzzing persistently. I awoke to an insistent alarm clock. And in elementary school I dreamed I ate a giant marshmallow and woke to find my pillow missing . . . nah! That was in a joke book I read in fourth grade.

Truths about our lives are often revealed through our dreams. Our guilt and longings, our obsessions, our fears, our desires. The great teacher and writer Don Murray of the University of New Hampshire published fiction earlier in his career. Here is a dream sequence from his 1964 novel, *The Man Who Had Everything*:

> Brad was gloriously aware of himself in the concentration of running, his head held up and the breeze self-made against his face, his chest large, his heart pumping, his lungs full, his arms following the hypnotic rhythm of his legs. He had his second wind and he felt he could go on forever as long as nothing broke the rhythm of his long legs, bare, his feet sockless

in the ankle-high moccasins that were soaked to the shape of his feet. They were quick to feel the contours of the earth, to seek a firm purchase, and then to spring his legs' power against the ground. He thrilled at the strength of his own legs—the muscles coiling and uncoiling, the strength of the matched thighs and calves, each doing its job of propelling him forward, up to the bend where the huge rock, lightning-cracked, stood, whirling by it and down the slope to the stream white-foamed with melted snow, almost falling pellmell down the slope, and then pulling up against the rise, reaching up and achieving the top, swinging right along the birch grove, following the road, enjoying the pain in his legs, their strength, the joy of running, until he woke, no longer a boy of fifteen but a man lying in the dark ward, immediately aware of where he was and hungering instantly for the freedom of the dream, which had been, for its few moments of eternity, so very real. (Murray 1964, 130–31)

At the end of the first chapter of *The Man Who Had Everything*, Brad becomes a paraplegic. The novel's central tension is Brad's struggle to accept his condition and live life productively, without bitterness and despair. It makes sense that to open one chapter, Murray describes a sensuous, triumphant dream of Brad doing what is lost to him forever.

After students have been immersed in their multigenre subject matter, I lead them into dreamwriting. I open a class by telling them, in detail, about dreams I have had. Sometimes I read from my notebook where I often write down my dreams, the most vivid ones when I've written soon after I've awakened and can recall more of the bizarre detail. Before I've talked long, students begin piping up with dreams of their own.

I ask them to take a few minutes to brainstorm their archive of memorable dreams. "When you strike a particularly vivid one," I say, "write every detail you remember." The more they write, the more of the dream comes available to them. We begin telling some of these dreams in class. I write the bones of each dream on the board. Dreamtalk begets more dreamtalk. I categorize the details they've recounted. Important people in their lives show up in dreams, ones they've known for years, like relatives or family friends; important people at particular times in their lives, like a coach or roommate;

or maybe people they haven't thought about in years. Certain places appear, activities or processes important to them, sports, work, play. Fears and anxieties are manifest. And lastly, their passions, desires, and obsessions influence the dreamscape.

In high school once, I dreamed of playing in a football game [obsession] on a muddy field on a Saturday afternoon [place], and being unable [fear] to throw [process] a touchdown pass we so desperately need to my friend and co-captain, Bill Jackson [person]. Our coach paces back and forth on the sideline, frowning. My friend Bill, sprinting downfield, turns into my girlfriend wearing her cheerleading uniform but I know she's really naked as she runs into the wind (forgot to mention that sex is often a part of dreams). My frowning coach on the sideline becomes my father clutching his chest as he did in 1957 when a heart attack nearly killed him. The football I hold in my right hand becomes a tiny pink pill, and I'm running for my life, barefoot. Just as much as I'm afraid I won't be able to throw the pill to my naked girlfriend, I'm afraid my feet will get stomped.

I know. A bizarre narrative. But in my dream it was perfectly normal, logical, real. At no time did my logical self step into the narrative and say, "Wait a minute. This is absurd. These things can't happen." No. Just as good fiction does, the dreamstory drives forward without explanation. When I awake, just like good fiction again, if there is meaning to be made of the bizarre sequence of events, I must make it. I must do the interpreting.

I have students choose one character involved in their multigenre papers. I list on the board these categories:

- passions, obsessions, desires
- fears, hauntings, anxieties
- key people in their lives
- processes or actions the character engages in

Students spend intense minutes retrieving details and information. Once they have a lot of data, if we have time, I might let them share with a partner for a few minutes to make the language pool richer. Then I lead students into the dream writing prompt:

Let the information you generated lead you. Let go, explore, invent, follow where language and images lead. Perhaps you'll latch onto a character's obsession as Don Murray did for Brad and write into it with all the senses alert. Maybe you'll describe surrealistic events as so many of our dreams were. Remember,

- Focus on your chosen character. Use first-person point of view or third person, whichever feels right, whichever you think most appropriate.
- The surreal is a distinct possibility. Be wildly flexible with time, place, characters, events, and imagery. There is no illogic in a dream. In fact, the illogical becomes logical.
- Passions, obsessions, fears, and anxieties come to the fore.
- Misfortune, aggression, tension are often present.
- Write with detail, images, drama, and *don't explain what anything means.* Let readers do the interpreting.
- Take ten to fifteen minutes. I'll write with you. Bear down and imagine.

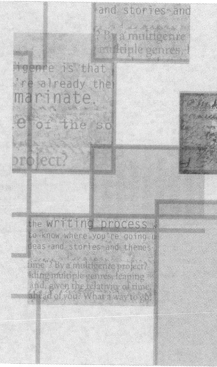

Here's what a dream piece in a multigenre paper *might* look like. The author was a student one summer at UNH in my multigenre class. She wrote about her relationship with her twin brother, whom she loved dearly. She was coming to terms, though, with the realization that over the years she had enabled his drug and alcohol addiction:

Recurring Dream

We're all in the backyard, friends and family, even people I don't recognize. The lawn is lush and immaculate except for one barren patch where the trampoline used to be. Everyone is laughing, barbequing, and playing badminton. I see Patrick from across the yard. He is eyeing the perfect blueness of the pool, a color he never remembers seeing before. The water is still and calm. He decides to dive in; water laps over the sides like an overfilled pot of boiling water. As I walk toward him, I notice the pool has frozen over, trapping him underneath. Frantic, I throw myself onto the ice and begin pounding it with my fists. The skin on my knuckles

breaks open, blood is dripping from my fingertips. I'm yelling. I'm scream-
ing. But no one comes to help. When I look up I see them; everyone is
pointing at me and laughing. Enraged, I continue to beat my fists against
the ice, but then I see something that stops me cold. From underneath
the frozen ice I see Patrick, he is pointing and laughing at me too.

Shannon Swiger, teacher

Sometimes students' dreamwrites morph into flashes or prose
poems. Sometimes the dream sparks the writer to create the counter-
dream of another character (Later in her paper, for example, Shannon
wrote a daydream her brother might have that revealed the hold and
danger of his addictions). As with writing a stream of consciousness,
dream writing works best when the writer lets go, follows language
where it leads, fleshes out images and associations that are suggested.

I'll leave you with the good advice that also came from Shannon
Swiger:

Different genres serve different purposes, and as the writer you need
to be cognizant of the power of each genre. I also think you need to be
flexible. For instance, if you're writing a poem and realize it's not working
and sounding more like a stream of consciousness, go for it. Make the
change. Often, the writing will lead you to the "right" genres.

25

Innovative Genres

Almost anything you do in the garden, for example weeding, is an effort to create some sort of order out of nature's tendency to run wild. There has to be a certain degree of domestication in a garden. The danger is that you can so tame your garden that it becomes a *thing*. It becomes landscaping.

In a poem, the danger is obvious; there is natural idiom and then there is domesticated language. The difference is apparent immediately when you sense everything has been subjugated, that the poet has tamed the language and the thought process that flows into a poem until it maintains a principle of order but nothing remains to give the poem its tang, its liberty, its force. (Kunitz 2007, 78)

Stanley Kunitz, poet

INSTEAD OF GARDENS AND POEMS, THE GREAT POET AND teacher could have been talking about the multigenre paper. It holds such possibility. It can head off in so many directions. There is no thesis, necessarily, to guide it down a particular highway and arrive at a certain destination. The multigenre paper and its process of creation are protean. The paper grows and changes under the hand of the writer, who sees what is needed and invents it. I'm not aware of any of my students who have outlined their multigenre papers and then simply written what was planned without discoveries and alteration during the making. "The multigenre paper you write," one of my students said, "is never the one you thought you would write."

Multigenre writers plan, write, plan anew, write more, revise, survey their production of genres, begin organizing them (I encourage students to lay their genres in order on the floor or a large table for an aerial view and moving pieces around as needed). They write new genres to fill gaps, realize suddenly that a new piece needs another piece to extend or counter it. The multigenre writing process is blissfully inventive. My writing prompts urge students along, spawning new writing and making discoveries. I keep students stirring the creative pot. Ingredients exchange flavors, grow rich in texture, variety, and meaning.

Such work alone, I'm convinced, will produce good multigenre papers. Without the writer's own inventiveness and imagination, however, the multigenre paper would lack tang, liberty, and force. Missing would be those surprises of language, form, and meaning that spring organically from the intense interaction of writer and subject matter. Often, the best parts of students' multigenre papers are pieces or writerly moves I could not have foreseen. As they worked with language—writing, revising, and envisioning—students became "harmonious with the material" (Stafford 1986, 63) and experienced "dawning realizations" (Stafford 1986, 60). They created genres I wish I'd known to ask for.

Melinda engaged both heart and mind and wrote a multigenre paper titled "The LD Student as Writer." Her younger brother of three years had been diagnosed as learning disabled. Through school he followed her with many of the same teachers, this girl who got A's, this girl who was dropped off for her first day of kindergarten and never looked back. Melinda had thrived. Her brother had not. He eventually quit school just weeks before his high school graduation. Melinda combined research into the literature of learning disabilities with field observations she'd done working in a middle school. And she was driven by burning, indelible memories of her brother's experience in education, what he had said about it, what she knew personally, and how she had seen his spirit flattened by school policies. In the piece below, she turns the standard textbook definition of "learning disabled" on its ear:

The Learning Abled: A Definition

The learning abled comprise approximately 100% of all students in the United States. The learning abled are characterized by a natural curiosity and desire to learn that may or may not be observable by middle childhood. Learning ability is a treatable condition. Treatments may include tracking, IEP's, learned helplessness, and poor educational experiences. Learning abled students respond well to environments in which they are treated as such, and will usually perform in direct correlation to the degree in which they are treated and addressed as a learning abled student.

Melinda Humbarger, college junior

Visuals

Matt is a high school English teacher who took my multigenre course through the Ohio Writing Project one summer. One of Matt's goals in "Open-Faced Sneezing Will Result in a Fine: The Influenza Pandemic of 1918" was to make vivid to readers the astounding scope of death worldwide caused by the flu: fifty million people in just one year. Matt learned that America lost more citizens to the 1918 flu than it had to World War I, World War II, and the wars in Korea and Vietnam, combined. What widened my eyes more, however, what drove home the catastrophic loss of human life across the globe that year was this visual Matt created with just a little bit of language to contextualize and stun you (see Figure 25–1).

Visual elements have become a staple of multigenre papers in my classes, once, that is, I, this word-man-of-a-teacher, got it through his head that visuals can often do what words cannot (or do them better). Visuals—photographs, maps, drawings, watercolors, collages, diagrams, charts, graphs, so much more—not only add aesthetic attractiveness but can also enhance and deepen meaning, if only students are given latitude to include images in their multigenre papers.

Figure 25–1:
Flu deaths worldwide

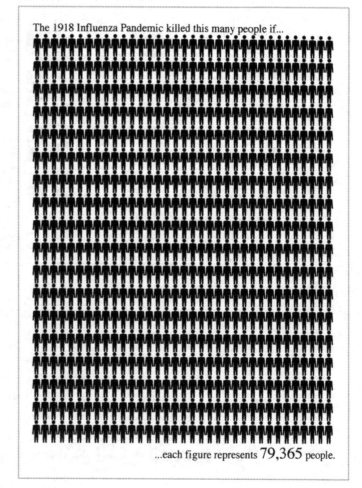

The 1918 Influenza Pandemic killed this many people if...

...each figure represents 79,365 people.

In writing about the sociology of the high school lunchroom, college sophomore Stacy Everson Garber created a "Seating Chart" (see Figure 25–2). Each table was precisely arranged and color-coded to match a legend, which indicated where each group sat. In one easily apprehended visual, Stacy reveals the social hierarchy of the lunchroom (and you thought lunch was just about tater tots).

Figure 25–2:
Lunchroom seating chart

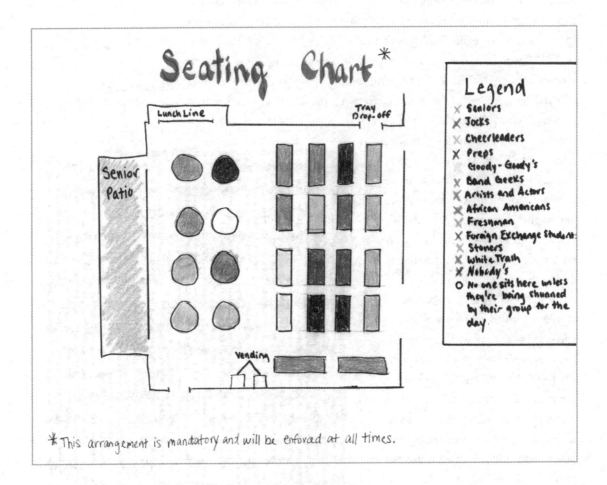

Carrie (Chapter 7), who investigated artistic expression and why and how children leave behind artistic ways of knowing as they progress through school, read research about the brain. One piece in her multigenre paper was this drawing she created in Figure 25–3.

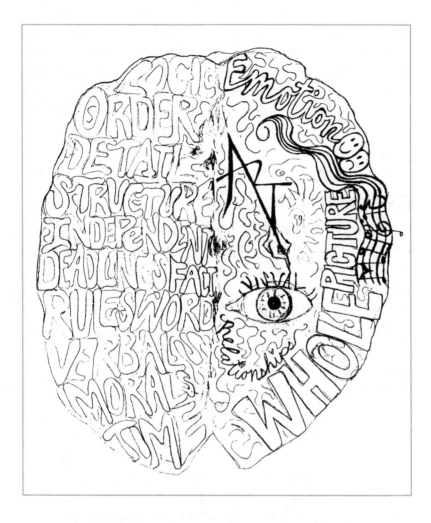

Figure 25–3: Brain

I'm one of those people whom Carrie laments. I drew as a child, even took art lessons for a year, had a house whose walls were covered with my mother's oil paintings. But I left art behind. Nothing in school asked me to continue growth in visual ways of knowing and communicating. I became a word man. The closest I come to using my spatial intelligence to make an appealing, functional visual, occurs each spring when I lay out the grid of my vegetable garden. Otherwise, I'm all about language. My loss. I have teacher friends, though, whose notebooks are combinations of exquisite handwriting and beautiful drawings. Although I can't resist lauding the skill of the art, I know that the important thing about drawing is not making beautiful pictures, but about using picture-making to think. The books of Karen Ernst (1993), Linda Rief (1998), and Roger Essley (2008) taught me that. I'll keep encouraging my methods students to capture some of their field observations with swift drawings, a way of seeing that many of them left behind in elementary school, as I did. And I'll keep requiring that students include visual elements in their multigenre papers.

Elegant Touches

Some of the most rewarding parts of multigenre papers I call "elegant touches": small, sometimes nuanced details that add to a paper's appeal, meaning, and aesthetic quality. For example, a first-year college student wrote about punk rock, its origin, history, characters and culture. Her elegant touch? She fastened the pages together with a safety pin.

Tori wrote a multigenre paper titled "Happily Ever After in the Media?" She used multigenre to examine how women are depicted, particularly in Disney movies. In the final paragraph of her "Dear Reader" introduction, she writes,

> Strong, independent women are not shown in fairy tales. Princesses never have jobs. Marriage is their only goal in life. Moreover, their lives are solely defined by the handsome men in the story. I do not mean to sound cynical because I am not. I watch Disney movies; I sing along to the songs; I think it's cute when the girls I baby-sit dress up like Belle and Cinderella. I see a place in our culture for fairy tales. Pretending and fantasizing are important parts of childhood. But, more importantly, I see a place for empowered women.

Six times in this multigenre paper of forty pages (she got into this project!), Tori includes a brief, sharp critique of a Disney movie. We might call them "Flash Reviews." Here is one:

The Little Mermaid Uncovered

> I understand that the seaweed is always greener in somebody else's lake. But could it really be green enough to leave your family and to permanently lose your voice? Luckily, as Ursula so poignantly reminds me (and young girls everywhere), men don't care about a woman's voice. In fact,

it's probably better in the long run, if women never speak again, right? Based on the fact that Eric tries to kiss Ariel without ever hearing her utter a word, Love is not based on personality, sense of humor or intellect. Love is apparently based on silence, submissiveness and a really good pair of legs.

Tori Grinberg, college junior

"Cinderella Uncovered," "Beauty and the Beast Uncovered," "Snow White Uncovered" . . . You get the idea. The elegant touch beyond Tori's effective repetition of form was this: Each movie critique appeared on a page alone. Behind the words was a watermark of the iconic Disney castle, complete with fireworks exploding above it. This almost subliminal image of fantasy, happiness, and possibility made Tori's critique, pragmatic eye, and biting humor all the more delicious.

Dedication

I remind students that major works of writing are often dedicated to someone important to the author. Salinger's *Catcher in the Rye* is dedicated "TO MY MOTHER." Capote's *In Cold Blood* to Jack Dunphy and Harper Lee. Cisneros' *House on Mango Street* to "*A las Mujeres*, To the Woman." Sometimes writers add language to identify the dedicatee. Donald Graves' groundbreaking book about teaching children to write, *Writing: Teachers and Children at Work*, held this dedication:

To
Donald M. Murray
writer, teacher, friend

Sometimes writers say more to indicate how they feel about the person the work is dedicated to, thinking, I guess, that dedicating a book to them is not enough. Herman Melville's dedication of *Moby Dick*:

In Token
of my admiration for his genius
This book is inscribed
to
Nathaniel Hawthorne

Ona Siporin wrote a more autobiographical, poetic dedication for *Stories to Gather All Those Lost*:

> To my Iowa family on that
> blacksatin bottomland farm along Indian Creek, who loved
> and nurtured the child, and to my husband and children, who
> have sustained the woman.

Sometimes the dedication is brief and poetic, as is Barbara Kingsolver's for *High Tide in Tucson*:

> for Steven,
> and every singing miracle

When I was finishing my first book, beginning the downward slope toward completion, I began to think about how I would write the "acknowledgments" and to whom I would dedicate *Clearing the Way*. I was so empty at that point I couldn't imagine writing another book, ever, so I made sure I dedicated it to the three most important people in my life:

> The hard, joyous work that was the writing of this book is dedicated to three women:
>
> My daughter, Mariana, who began teaching me to see soon after she started talking.
>
> My wife, Kathy, who has survived much, grown strong, and remained loving.
>
> My mother, Mae, who won an essay contest in 1930 when she was fifteen. She had written about pottery making, a subject her family knew well. When asked to read her essay, she did and grew increasingly pale and terrified as she stood before her classmates on that, the last day she ever attended school.

I suggest to students that they might want to dedicate their papers to someone. For most of them, it has never crossed their minds to dedicate a paper written for a school assignment. Multigenre, of course, is no ordinary school assignment. This is an opportunity, I tell them, to pay respect, gratitude, and love. Some students make the most of it, as Chelsea Donavan did for "Living Thin: One Girl's Fight for a **Full Life**":

> I dedicate this multigenre paper to my body.
> The body, that no matter at what weight it was, has carried me through my life without fail. It has healed and bounced back from heartbreak and weakness, it has walked great distances, and—most importantly—it has danced. Please, take this as my apology. I will try to look at you and treat you better. Thank you for working with me even when I don't.

IV

Prime Spots

Everything matters in writing, even something so
small as deciding where to put a comma, choosing
a better verb, or deciding to fasten together the
pages of your multigenre paper about punk rock
with a safety pin. There are prime spots, however,
critical places in a multigenre paper that I take care
to alert students to and teach the best I can.

26

Don't
Dis the
Beginning

THOSE FIRST WORDS READERS' EYES TOUCH, THE FIRST sentence, the first paragraph, the first page, the initial opportunity for readers to synchronize with the writer's voice, stance, and subject matter . . . nothing is more important. I don't care if it's a job application, a poem, a dissertation. Nothing is more important than the beginning. Nothing—until, of course, readers are beyond it, and the writer has won their good will.

As a reader, I want to be captivated. I *need* to be captivated. I want the writing to pique my interest, rouse my curiosity, pleasure me with language. I want a sense that the writer will be taking me somewhere. I confess I've started novels I stopped reading because of tedious, meandering beginnings. As a teacher I read reams of student papers. I read them regardless of their craft, but it's not good for me and not good for students when their lead has me frowning and disbelieving within a minute. That isn't like me. Before I read the first word, I'm an optimist, wanting to believe, ready to be carried away, eager to head down the page to hear a new voice and see what I can learn. But if writers do something early on that repels me and squanders this fresh start, they lose my good will.

The first piece of writing in multigenre papers holds double responsibility. The paper is so far from traditional research papers, so unexpected by readers that multigenre writers must take care not to lose them or alienate them on that opening page. The paper must hook readers intellectually (and, I would argue, emotionally). It must ground them with vital information they'll need to build meaning as they travel deeper into the topic, holding increasing complexity in their heads. I want multigenre writers to take me by the hand, hold it firmly, and let me glimpse the vista ahead.

As a member of academia, I am all too familiar with introductions, prefaces, prologs and the like that warn readers away, rather than invite them in. The opening language is verbose or throat clearing or pompous or so concerned with backstory, previous research, and appearing learned that I lose steam in my reading. My good will is crushed, and I begin flipping pages to see how long this puppy is. I'm not talking only about educational research. I've run down my battery reading long-winded, scholarly introductions that an editor thought was a good idea to place in front of the first page of a novel, even a great novel, which *may* have been suitable for fellow academics but not for general, flesh and blood readers who want to get on with the story.

After students' research is well underway and they've been writing multiple genres, I spend part of a class period talking about beginnings, openings, first impressions and showing them samples. The time is right for such talk. Weeks of reading, writing, and thinking about their topics have worked a synergy. Unbidden, it seems, students have begun to imagine an architecture for their papers. That first piece of writing—that entryway—must extend an invitation to read they cannot refuse. How, I want students to consider, can I begin my multigenre paper in a compelling way? I have them jot down what readers ought to know up front in order to read with purpose and growing hunger to know more.

To this end, English teacher, Patty Cavuoto, an avid outdoorswoman, began her multigenre paper with a tale that might make you squirm, which led into a brief "Dear Reader," all this occurring on page 1:

My friend told me this story once about when he hiked The Long Trail. He went swimming in one of the many lakes to cool off, and then he, eventually, went to bed. He woke up sometime in the middle of the night, his ears clogged. Thinking he had swimmer's ear, he shook his head, banging his temples to loosen the water. But it wouldn't unclog. His head was getting muffled, and he couldn't sleep. Then all of a sudden.

This whirring sound echoed inside his head.

Whirr whirr whirr.

It was deafening. He got out the med kit for the Q-tips. As he stuck one in, the whirring got louder and louder, and he felt something that just couldn't be water in his ear.

Whirr, whirr, whirr.

Confused and a little frightened, he took the Q-tip out. Something that looked like a black fuzzy leg was hanging on the tip of the swab. He resisted the thought of what that meant. He grabbed the bottle of rubbing alcohol and poured it in his ear.

The whirring turned to a screech.

He grabbed more Q-tips and jabbed them in his ear, one by one he pulled out seven more black fuzzy legs to confirm that what was living in his ear was, in fact, a spider.

Dear Reader . . .

The following is not about spiders. But it very well could be. No, the following passages trace the journey I took through the Green Mountains of Vermont on a path called The Long Trail. Through these short snippets you will get a feel of what it's like to be a long-distance hiker and to show you what really happens out on the trail. I can't make you sweat while reading. I can't make the bugs gnaw at your skin, and I can't make you feel hunger like I did, but I will try and make you feel like you are sweating, that the bugs are biting you, and that you go away hungry for more.

Patty Cavuoto, teacher

I love Patty's combination of creepy story and plainspoken prognostication of what is in store for readers (although I can't help wanting to stick my little finger in my ear and gouge it out).

How about a fanciful beginning? In "Viva Viola" a first-year music major writes about her central passion. To begin her paper, she puts on a mask, giving voice to her beloved instrument. The inanimate object becomes a character, telling us about itself from a first-person point of view, setting us up to learn more about its history, capabilities, sound, and place:

Dear Reader,

I am not my pesky little brother. I am not my graceful older sister. I can define myself without the others. I am not useless or meaningless. I am deep, mysterious, educated, patient. A good soul. You do not notice me, many do not know me, but if I am gone you will miss me.

I am the viola. I express the soul in a way no one else can. Bigger, better, and lower than my brother violin, my sound is foreboding beneath the ear of my player as it grows, overcoming the player and audience. I play notes that have a dark color, though I can and do expand to be bright and festive.

I am strong and challenging. My size (larger than little brother violin) makes me difficult to play on the shoulder. I require dedication, skill and agility. My solo works from the last century take great skill as I continually challenge.

I am unique. You don't know how to deal with me because I often shatter my label. I am not dull witted, foolish, or incapable. I am not slow. I am a virtuoso—an esoteric that once discovered is loved by all. I am the joy in students' life as they discover the sound within. I add something to music no others can. As one violist of the Toledo (OH) symphony said, "In a dessert, I, the viola, am the cinnamon. A spice that adds just the right touch. A spice you miss if it's gone."

Legend tells I developed first of my family. Viola. Violin, as a diminutive, means "little viola." I'm older, different and more complex than my brother violin. My register is a deep green, a rich purple. I can be golden. A striking red most heartbreaking sunset of your life or most meaningful moment, the climax of your life.

K. Jean Forney, college freshman

I know little about classical music and the viola, but I'm pleased with what I've learned from this voice that's so companionable. I'm eager to learn more.

I've had students who have taken even more risk with how they began their papers. One student wrote about a topic he was presently surviving: the shock and adjustment to his first year of college. It had sobered and tested him. Here is the first piece readers encounter:

DEAN OF ADMISSIONS WARNING: Attending college has been known to cause one or more of the following: homesickness, clogging of communication lines, role strain, decreased circulation to the heart, increased circulation to the brain, growth of semi-philosophical tumors which can impair brain functioning and fine motor skills, insomnia, increased social supports, severe change in dietary habits, foot in mouth disease, higher societal pressure, impaired judgment during late hours, eye strain, facebook addiction, carpal tunnel, ideological congestion, writer's elbow, heavy doses of perspective, insomnia, increased risk of cancer if cell phone use does in fact cause it, diarrhea, delusions of future grandeur, homesickness, development of violent alter-egos that emerge only in 32-bits, dissociative disorder, decreased automobility and mono.

Nicholas Masso, college freshman

And then there is simply directness, clarity, and a clear understanding that the stakes of what you are about to read are high. Those leads get me to turn the page every time. Liz was a first-year student when she wrote "Laugh So You Don't Cry: A Personal Account of Alzheimer's Disease." Before her "Dear Reader," on the same page, she places a revealing anecdote and then expands upon it to discuss her theme:

While putting on my coat to leave church on Sunday, I saw Grandpa don a black overcoat. I thought nothing of this until Grandma walked up to him and said, "Forrest, you didn't wear a coat today." She helped him out of it, smiling. "Oh no, you're stealing jackets again. I told you to stop doing that at church. You can steal jackets at a restaurant, no one knows us there."

Dear Reader,

My grandfather has Alzheimer's disease. Don't worry. You're not a horrible person for laughing at the above story. Many, many people have to deal with this devastating disease, and they have different ways of dealing with it. Personally, I have found humor to be especially effective. It's not that I'm making fun of my grandpa. I'm just trying to deal. We're all just trying to deal.

As situations like this become more and more frequent, it has become necessary to adopt a new worldview. You know, sometimes you have to laugh. You have to laugh so you don't cry. You have to focus on the good so you can deal with the bad.

This past summer, my mother, my little sister, my grandparents, and I spent three weeks in Canada at our cabins on Lake Huron. I go up every year but have never stayed for that long. This year, for the first time, we couldn't leave my grandparents alone. Up until that trip, I didn't know that my grandfather had Alzheimer's. It was a tough summer, one that I will always remember.

This paper is about Alzheimer's disease. About what my grandfather is going through. About what I'm going through. About what we're all going through. And about how we can handle living with such a terrible affliction and keep our senses of humor intact.

Cheers,

Liz Miller, college freshman

That first piece of writing in a multigenre paper, whether you call it "Dear Reader," "Introduction," or "Prolog," whether you dive right in to your very first genre without explanation, as Nicholas Masso did, with faith that its title and content will heighten readers' interest, whatever the lead piece is, whatever you call it, don't waste the opportunity to make a strong first impression, to ground readers with what they need, to lure them into your multigenre paper where you will reward them with a fulfilling reading experience full of surprises of language, information, and insights.

And whether you purposefully conjure a beginning, brainstorming first what readers need up front, deciding how much you will tell—as Jean does with "Viva Viola"—or whether you just write your heart out, experimenting with one genre after another and find that you stumble upon a piece that—with a little shaping and tinkering—will perfectly open your paper . . . however you arrive at your beginning, know that it's a prime spot and know that readers will appreciate you crafting it.

27

Of Golden Threads and Unity

"I Remember That!"

This multigenre paper is turning out to be more difficult than I imagined. I love vampires, I know a lot about them, I enjoy learning more about them, so I thought I'd be able to pump this paper out with no problem whatsoever. The difficulty here is that it's hard to weave my pieces together to make one continuous, coherent paper. I understand that that's the point, to write in different styles and connect them to present a topic in an interesting, cohesive way. That, however, is easier said than done.

Suzanne Evans, college senior

The one thing that surprised me the most about this project was how the multigenre paper seemed to come together on its own. When I started doing research into "happiness" and writing pieces, I wasn't sure exactly where I was headed. The paper spoke to me, and all I had to do was discover the pattern it was telling me and utilize it.

Lina Aukstuolis, college sophomore

SUZANNE WAS A CAPABLE WRITER, A NO-NONSENSE WRITER, A direct, accessible, inspired writer. Maybe she was pressing too hard to unify her paper. And maybe Lina was naïve about multigenre, too easily accepting and optimistic, not fully cognizant of the obstacles in the path ahead—she was, after all, writing about "happiness." Both women, though, through their immersion and right minds found ways to unify their informative, funny, sophisticated multigenre papers.

The unity and cohesiveness writers can achieve in multigenre papers might be their most rewarding feature, the one that moves multigenre toward art. One of my friends calls unity and cohesiveness an organic quality that grows naturally out of the subject matter. I don't believe I've ever taught a student who planned unifying elements for her paper prior to beginning it. Such ideas usually arise during the heat of composing and immersion in a topic, the yin-yang thinking processes of intense engagement and alternate subconscious mulling when we are otherwise occupied (while swimming for me). During the weeks students create their papers, I'm in there pedagogically pitching, throwing strikes about how students might achieve unity, showing them examples from past students' work. It comes down to a rule of nature and art: "Repetition," said Stanley Kunitz, "can unify an experience" (Kunitz 2007, 74).

Film Interlude

I show students a three-minute excerpt from the Marx Brothers' *Animal Crackers* (1930). It's black and white, made just three years after sound movies made their debut with *The Jazz Singer* (1927), another opportunity to teach and conserve a bit of American culture. One character in the movie is a pompous art collector. Chico has a hunch the man is a fraud and finally remembers his identity: Abe Kabibble, not an art collector at all, but a former fish peddler from Czechoslovakia. He can prove his hunch by locating Kabibble's prominent birthmark, though he can't remember where it was located. Chico and Harpo wrestle the man to the floor, search thoroughly, and find the silver dollar-sized birthmark on his forearm. Kabibble offers Chico and Harpo a bribe to keep quiet about his identity. They want the bribe increased. After hilarious banter, slapstick, and unsuccessful negotiation, Kabibble storms off. Chico reveals that amid the mayhem he has stolen the man's necktie. "Whadda you got?" he asks Harpo. Harpo pulls back his sleeve—the birthmark!

Students' laughter is spontaneous. They had forgotten the birthmark and were delighted at its reappearance. The comedic scene dramatically illustrates the essence of unity in multigenre papers: repetition and surprise.

Repetition, Surprise, and a Golden Thread

As much as we cherish surprises and newness, we would sorely miss a world without repetition. The seasons repeat, traditions repeat, cycles of sleep and renewal repeat. For teachers and students, the beginnings and endings of school years repeat. Our breathing, our heartbeats, our walking upon the earth, all are dependent upon repetition. Writers, too, repeat as they engage in craft. They repeat words, details, images, themes. A novelist introduces a character, develops her role in the plot, leaves her for a time. We read on, engrossed in the story. When the character reappears, we are surprised and rewarded. Writing gains power and depth through repetition. Poets and essayists tell us something in the first stanza or paragraph. In the last stanza or conclusion, that very information, detail, or image comes zinging home to us. We find ourselves nodding our heads or wiping tears from our eyes: this because of the meaning, of course, meaning often brought home through skillful repetition.

My daughter, Mariana Romano, teaches English at Evanston Township High School, immediately north of Chicago. Each semester in her senior English classes, she has students write multigenre papers about the last two novels they read—it serves as their semester exam. One semester she pairs Tim O'Brien's *The Things They Carried* (1990) with Kurt Vonnegut's *Slaughterhouse Five* (1969). The next semester she pairs Kate Chopin's *The Awakening* (1899) with Zora Neale Hurston's *Their Eyes Were Watching God* (1937). Mariana requires students to include in their papers what she calls a "golden thread," a unifying element that appears in some of the genres that binds the theses students have created between the two novels. One student, for example, developed the thesis of the rise of the antihero that she saw clearly dramatized in O'Brien's and Vonnegut's novels. Her golden thread was the imagery of comic book heroes.

Such repetition, such stitching in of a golden thread, takes multigenre beyond merely a portfolio of diverse pieces of writing about the same topic. "I wrote a multigenre paper in high school," one student told me, "but each genre was specifically assigned. I paid little attention to the power of their interaction." It's a good idea, I think, for students to write about a topic through different lenses. But it's not multigenre. The point, Suzanne wrote in the epigram, is "to write in different styles and connect them to present a topic in an interesting, coherent way."

When writers seek to create unity in their multigenre papers—whether that quest comes easily as Lina reported or with difficulty as Suzanne admitted—the writer experiences pleasures: the pleasure of sudden insight, the pleasure of creating order from chaos, the pleasure of spontaneity, the pleasure of thinking with the whole mind. It's not the thrill of a fifty-yard touchdown pass or of one backstroker out-touching another, but its pretty good living. We need to exhort students to take note of these quiet achievements, these small pleasures that occur during the process of writing, which includes time away from direct word work, when subject matter is composting in our subconscious. I don't know anyone who writes with purpose who doesn't appreciate and respect this magic.

Soon after students have begun their projects—maybe two weeks into the work—I introduce them to the concept of *repetend*—when writers repeat a key word, phrase, sentence, or longer element in a piece of writing. I give students a list of ways they might unify their papers:

1. Repeat an image, a detail, or exact language.

In one of his masterpieces, *Rebecca* (1940), director Alfred Hitchcock repeats the image of a cursive *R*, which, we soon realize, conjures the deceased, mysterious, first wife of Max de Winter, whom one character describes as "the most beautiful creature" he'd ever seen. (*Creature* appears to be the right word: self-centered, amoral, ravenous.) Hitchcock never shows us a portrait or photo of Rebecca, yet we see her vividly through what various characters say about her, the factual details we learn of her life, the things she left behind after her sudden death. Periodically, Hitchcock settles the camera briefly on the image of that cursive *R*: on a handkerchief, an address book, a napkin, a blanket, embroidered with flourish on a pillowcase. Each appearance of the *R* is subtle, surprising, haunting. Great literature, too, of course, features the repetition of ideas and key language. In *Slaughterhouse-Five*, that novel so full of death and humor, whenever someone or something dies—whether bubbles bursting on the surface of champagne or six million Jews in Nazi death camps—Kurt Vonnegut writes, "So it goes," as Tralfamadorians say to reflect their practical view of death. And what was it that Sam-I-Am kept prodding the narrator to eat? Nine different times amid a flurry of rhyme? (I will not say it. I will not. You enter memory and give it some thought.)

Four More Ways to Achieve Unity

2. Repeat a pattern of quotations, pictures, or titles.

In her multigenre paper about Marilyn Monroe, a high school student chooses photographs of Marilyn from various points in her life to coincide with each genre she's written, every one of which bears the title of a Monroe movie. At the bottom of the page each genre is followed with a pertinent quotation from Monroe that enhances the meaning of the writing. In another paper, a teacher writes a multigenre response to a book. After the title of each piece, she includes a quotation from the author that touches on the theme of what you are about to read.

3. Repeat a form, genre, or style.

Six times interspersed strategically through her multigenre paper about Alzheimer's disease and her grandfather's decline, Liz imagines her grandfather's thoughts through brief, impressionistic interior monologs. To get close to representing thought, she writes in an unpunctuated, anxiety-ridden inner speech that grows progressively more jumbled with each piece. In "Happy Ever After in the Media?" Tori creates six examples of her "uncovered" reviews of Disney movies about female characters, placing them strategically throughout the paper. And Jamie uses four expository pieces about the inception and history of punk rock, titled: "Opening Act," "First Set," "Second Set," and "Encore." They "are meant to be parts of a whole," she explains. "I divided them and distributed them throughout the paper so that information would come as it was needed, and also to provide a truer sense of the passage of time through the punk movement." In "A More Scientific Explanation of Happiness," Lina uses Diener's "Satisfaction with Life Scale" (Diener 2001), filled out five times by the same fictional character, at sixteen, twenty-three, forty-three, sixty-seven, and eighty-three. (The sixty-seven-year-old turns out to be the most content.)

4. Repeat a scene from a different point of view.

In writing about the 2001 racial unrest in Cincinnati sparked by the death of a twenty-year-old black man at the hands a police officer, Melissa writes an interior monolog of those seconds of the chase and gunshot from the first-person point of view of the victim. Sixteen pages later, she writes another interior monolog of those same seconds, this time from the police officer's point of view. Each piece begins with the sentence "The night is pitch" and then reveals the perceptions, feelings, fears, and motives of the narrators. The effect is to humanize both characters and complicate the truth of what happened that night.

5. Write a precise, significant fragment of a scene, memorable for its language, imagery, and content. Later, surprise readers with a rendering of the fully developed scene repeating some of that memorable language, imagery, and content.

When multigenre writers achieve this effect, readers are rewarded with answers to events or dialog they hadn't quite grasped earlier. Michael Ondaatje famously did this in *The Collected Works of Billy the Kid* (1970). On page 12 he describes an outlaw being ambushed, shot as he steps through a doorway. It's just a fragment from Billy's point of view, only eight lines. Ten pages later—after nine genres have intervened—Ondaatje renders in third person on one page an expanded narrative of the scene with key words, images, and phrases repeated from the fragment. The effect is to be simultaneously repelled by the matter of fact violence of the scene and dazzled by Ondaatje's artistry.

One Example of a Writer Creating a Golden Thread

Here's one way this attention to repetend, unity, and cohesion played out in one of my students: Ellen wrote "The Rose: A Multigenre Paper on Connecting with Loved Ones Lost." Her inquiry was sparked by the loss two years earlier of her grandmother when Ellen was studying abroad. In much of the paper, Ellen uses multiple genres and eight photographs to bring details of her grandmother to life on the page: her striking Irish beauty, fondness for Capri pants, red lipstick, "doing" lunch, a longstanding book club, her can-do upbeat spirit, and her attitude of living deeply and freely in every aspect of life. Ellen's paper goes beyond a character sketch, though. She investigates the enduring nature of love, its power, its persistence. After her grandmother's passing, Ellen believed there had been signs from her, indicating that she was at peace and watching over those she loved. In her "Dear Reader" Ellen writes, "Love is the bridge that connects us to each other—across the miles, across the years, and even across the barrier of death."

On page 19, after her grandmother has passed, Ellen renders this dream:

"Help!" I screamed. "Please somebody help me!"

I could feel its hot, sweaty breath; it smelled like foul waste. I dug my nails through the snow and into the hard ground. With each shriek I let out, its eyes grew darker. With every plea for help, it grew more massive. Soon it was looming overhead, blocking what was left of my view of the moon. I could see my reflection in its eyes. I broke into a cold sweat. I prayed to feel numb. I didn't want to feel its teeth sinking into my flesh. I tried to scream but now nothing came out. I tried to run, but the walls of the snow bank were too steep, too tall. I was trapped. I could see my route of escape just over the snow bank walls but I couldn't reach it. Its fur was grey and white. Its whiskers looked like knives that could skin me alive. It was a wolf.

Just at it opened its jaw to devour me an image came into my mind. A picture of my grandma, laughing and running down the stairs in her Capri pants. She was smiling and nodding, as if to say that everyone would be all right. All right? A wolf was about to tear me apart and she was nodding in approval? But for some reason I felt better, warmer. I felt safe. I wasn't scared anymore. The wolf didn't look the same to me and I began to hear its breathing again, the thudding of my heart in my ears finally subsiding. And then, after this roller coaster of emotion . . . I woke up. It had all been a dream. But why had I thought of my Grandma? And why was there a wolf in my dream? I would wait two weeks before the answer dawned on me. The answer was worth waiting for.

Ellen Conrad, college junior

Readers keep this indelible wolf-dream filed away in memory. Eight pages later—after poems, expository pieces, an account of a near-miss auto accident, a recounting of a strange experience at Mass one-year-to-the-day after her grandmother's passing—you encounter this page:

A wolf lives in a pack, a family oriented structure. Wolves communicate with each other more by harmony and integration than by aggression and submission. My grandma was a part of a women's book club called "The Wolves." For 15 years they met twice a month and talked about books and their families. They saw each other through happy times of grand-children being born and the sad times of husbands passing away. When my grandma got sick, they were there for her. They drove her to doctors' appointments. They moved the meeting times to whenever she felt up to them. They were her rock. My grandma loved The Wolves, and I loved them because they were there in a way I couldn't be.

Below and to the right of this bit of exposition was a small color photo Ellen had found, a close up of two wolves nose to nose. At the bottom of the page, this:

Cold snow.
  No escape.
    Heart panicking.
      The wolf.
        Fear.
          And then a presence.
            Trust.
              Safety.
                It was her.

If we'd had time for one more revision, I'd have asked Ellen to consider cutting the last five sentences of the dream description. I think it would lead to a better payoff for readers if she does not tip her hand that there will be an explanation for the unsettling, yet calming nightmare. Regardless, I was delighted to see the writing craft Ellen employed. She'd put indelible images in my mind, left them for a time, then returned to them to bring home meaning.

I wrote in *Blending Genre, Altering Style* (2000) that getting students to achieve unity in their multigenre papers was the most difficult part of teaching students to write them. I don't think that anymore. Although teaching unity requires our good faith work, it's fun to help students develop that golden thread. Collecting a set of multigenre papers and seeing the varied ways students have achieved unity is a distinct payoff for you, the writing teacher, hunched over a desk at God knows what hour.

28

Another Rhetorical Space

To My Colleagues in the Field

When that certain grounder
skips blur-white
across clipped June grass

and I move quick but bobble it
the ball popping into the air before my eyes
I need you moving to cover second

timing my work while the ball's between us
ready to take my toss
tap the bag in stride

and wheel your own true throw to first
in time
you and I will teach the world

to collaborate [Note 1]

THAT POEM WAS WRITTEN DURING A TIME I WAS STUDYING collaborative learning, beyond, "Yeah, put the kids in groups!" Collaboration was more than people working together to complete a job. Collaboration led to learning and growth when people of different skills and abilities worked together, when Vygotsky's Zone of Proximal Development kicked in. Collaboration also offered a chance for participants to work in that Intermental Development Zone, "where the collective intellect in which a student is participating manages to accomplish things that the solitary intellect cannot" (Johnston 2004, 69). I was learning that others—artists, scholars, craftspeople, filmmakers, philosophers, writers—are "distant teachers" (John-Steiner 1985), though we never meet them or sit in their classrooms. Those distant teachers collaborate with us in our endeavor to learn.

At the same time I had a draft of "To My Colleagues in the Field," I was under the spell of a distant teacher named Georgia Heard through her classic book about teaching children to write poetry, *For the Good of the Earth and Sun* (1989). In one section Georgia writes about white space, particularly the white space created when a poem appears in stanzas: Poets may use white space to make a break in the information or thought of a stanza; to slow the poem down; to encourage the reader to stop and reflect after a thought; to make the poem look more orderly; to set off the poem's final line and give it more impact; or to single out a line by surrounding it in silence (Heard 1989, 63–64).

Upon reading that section, I rose abruptly from my chair, went to my desk, and experimented with adding white space to the solid block of lines I'd written. That burst of creativity—spurred by words of a distant teacher—was exhilarating. I not only grouped lines into stanzas but also changed line breaks and tinkered with language. The poem I ended with looked aesthetically different. It was easier to read, too, something I'm always shooting for. And I loved deciding to place the final two words in a separate line by themselves, apart from the words above them, collaborating with each other, so to speak.

I want my students to have the experience in their multigenre research of collaborating with distant teachers, or as one scholar calls them, "intellectual allies" (Newkirk 2009, 12). The thinking of those allies sparks our own thinking, strengthens our resolve, and, in the case of multigenre, can provide both the grounding and impulse for creativity. As a teacher interested in process as well as product, I want to know about my students' learning journeys. In addition to students compiling a scholarly "Works Cited" page, they must also write notes about their work. They can use a footnoting format or create a section at the end, calling it "Notes," "Note Page," or "Endnotes."

An example: Emily studied for licensure in our Master of Arts in Teaching program. She inquired into the education of tween girls, titling her paper "A Moment That Is Mine: Girls in the Language Arts Classroom." Her inquiry was driven by the memory of her own tween years and what journal writing had meant to her and two of her friends. In her introduction she writes,

> We were female Holdens, you might say. We were tormented with the injustice of adolescence and frightened by our upcoming transition to adulthood. That year we kept journals. Not because any teacher said we should, but because we needed to. We needed to work out our feelings on paper. Most importantly, we shared our writing with one another.

Emily read books, websites, position papers, poetry, and articles from newspapers and professional journals. Her "Works Cited" page was a banquet of sources for the topic. Here is one brief monolog from her multigenre paper:

How I Became a Writer in the Sixth Grade

> I stood before 25 pairs of critical eyes and wondered what to do. Stared at my paper, sighed, and began reading my work. So scared, but proud of what I had written. My first poem that mattered. Race relations in the school. Sixth grade. About the second line I really got rollin'. Performed. I beamed red of embarrassment. And excitement. And pride. And the knowledge that the cheers and clapping had me hooked. A talent for words. Words that meant something.

Here is the corresponding entry in Emily's Endnotes:

> "How I Became a Writer in the Sixth Grade" was inspired by *In Our Own Words: Students' Perspectives on School*. This book shares the experience of various teens in school. One chapter, called "Writing the Wrong: Making Schools Better for Girls," is devoted to the importance of free writing and journaling for adolescent girls. One girl wrote about her experience with sharing what she wrote, the praise she received from peers, and how she felt like she became a writer that day. This piece shows the importance of peer acceptance and the community of writers that needs to be established in the classroom so that girls will feel validated and believe in their work.

One of the great multigenre teachers in the land, Nancy Mack of Wright State University has called endnotes "another rhetorical space" (2006, 71). An entry in a notes section offers students a chance to elaborate a point, discuss further research, clarify ambiguity, place the genre in a larger context, and—one of my favorites as a curious teacher—reveal the creative process. Students can, in effect, use the endnotes as a rhetorical space to create anew.

All that said, I have two caveats about endnotes.

One of my students objected to adding notes and internal citations to the multigenre paper:

I am undecided about the Endnotes. While I think it is good to explain your thought process, I felt that the Endnotes took away from the project. Maybe it goes back to what I said before about being able to create my own meaning without the author's opinions or conclusions to muddle my thoughts. I like the projects for their aesthetics and content, not the motivation behind the pieces the author wrote.

Elizabeth Marshall, college junior

I'm sympathetic to Elizabeth's point. For *The Collected Works of Billy the Kid*, Michael Ondaatje wrote only a brief "Credits," listing four sources and telling what parts of his book were derived from them, concluding with this passage: "With these basic sources I have edited, rephrased, and slightly reworked the originals. But the emotions belong to their authors" (Ondaatje 1970, unnumbered final page). The bulk of multigenre features narrative thinking—poetry, fictional narrative, dramatic dialog, and imaginative hybrid genres. We wouldn't think of requiring poets, novelists, and playwrights to explain what they have done in their writing. Multigenre requires students to work in genres that are by definition implicit.

And yet, I am a teacher, not an editor. I'm not just picking up students' work in a bookstore or buying it online. I want to know the ins-and-outs of students' learning and creative journeys. I want students to be academically responsible and practice the habit of scholarly integrity. So I ask them to include endnotes. Initially, I was assertive and demanding in my requirement. In a memo to students I wrote,

Each piece ought to have something written about it in an endnotes section. You might tell how research informed the piece or the function it plays in the paper. You might describe the creation of the piece, if that will further inform the reader.

Since I'd made such a big deal about endnotes, students rightly inferred that my *ought* really meant *must*. Did I ever pay the price! Every paper in that batch of fifty contained interesting information about *some* of the pieces. In most of the papers, however, students went on and on in the endnotes, blathering about banalities, filling up the rhetorical space with wordswordswords because Romano surely wanted endnotes whether there was anything pertinent to say or not. I made that mistake only once. I want endnotes, I tell students now, but I want them to be relevant and meaningful. I want them to offer genuine insight.

A Ghost from Teaching Past

Jonathan Graham was a high school senior the first year I had students write multigenre papers. He wanted to be a playwright, and he had the talent, perceptivity, and drive to accomplish it. On one of his papers I wrote, "Jonathan, I'm sure that one day you will make your daily bread by writing." And he has, making a living for over a decade now as a writer and editor. For his multigenre paper as a high school senior, Jonathan wrote about Tennessee Williams, creating scenes, monologs, diary entries, letters, newspaper reviews, and poems. Sometimes Jonathan included direct passages from his research in his brilliant multigenre paper.

The following year at Beloit College, Jonathan worked more with that paper and submitted it to the English Department's David and Marion Stocking Prize for "best non-fiction prose by a student." The judge was a writer and professor at another small liberal arts college. In a written note, the judge gently admonished Jonathan that if he ever wrote this kind of paper again to be clearer about his sources . . . and then he awarded Jonathan the prize!

The teenagers in Jonathan's class had read my passions. They knew I was all about creativity and expression. I had said plenty about that, but little about responsible scholarship. When Jonathan visited the high school over a break, he told me what had happened. I was embarrassed, felt I had shortchanged this young man. Years later, I realized that endnotes, not just "acknowledgments" or "credits" as Ondaatje had written, would have prevented the judge's confusion about his paper. If I'd been more thoughtful about the multigenre project in those early years, if I'd demonstrated concern about authorship and possible perceptions of plagiarism, I would have been a better teacher. Jonathan would have learned how helpful to readers endnotes could be, how they could clarify, extend, inform, and complicate. I wasn't there yet. Jonathan, here is my apology, just a quarter century late.

Endnotes

1. Note 1, page 150, "To My Colleagues in the Field": This poem got its start in an argument I was having with another teacher. He was indignant about students' lack of skills and knowledge. He blamed their previous teachers. My position was that teachers across grade levels had to work together to teach students. We teach the best we can, students learn what they learn, then the next teacher goes to work. At one point in the argument, I blurted, "When I catch the ball, I need you covering second." The sentence so surprised me that I surprised my arguing partner by immediately withdrawing a 3 x 5 card from my breast pocket and jotting down the metaphor.

The idea of teacher collaboration relates directly to Penny Rief's apocryphal study, *Curriculum Design and Student Achievement*. The author writes persuasively that teachers need to meet across grade levels and communicate to each other what they seek to teach their students. Just as good infielders do when they turn a double play, teachers must work together.

I must also admit that I like my title's play on words with *baseball field* and *field of teaching*.

Evaluation and Reflection

These siblings lead to more fully realized multigenre papers and fairer grading on the teacher's part. Discussed in this section are the reality, practicality, and myth of rubrics, the gaping hole in the Common Core Standards, and the fit of multigenre for our multigenre lives.

Evaluation and Learning

I was confounded by the amount of adequate but not stellar writing that was getting rave reviews by my rubric. Sure the students could follow directions and make a functional essay. But none of them were writing with the gusto to knock me on the seat of my pants.

Jennifer Gunther, graduate student

I HAVE A LINE I OFTEN USE NEAR THE END OF WORKSHOPS about multigenre when an inevitable question arises. By that time most of the teachers are engaged and interested. Those who know multigenre are thinking of ways to tweak what they do. Those who don't know multigenre are imagining possibilities for their students. Someone asks, "How do you evaluate multigenre papers?"

"Thanks for coming today," I say. "I'm afraid we're out of time."

Brief laughter. I've just suggested what many teachers wish they could do: avoid evaluation. Regardless of subject area, many of us grapple with evaluation: We want to be rigorous, yet fair; we want to set high standards, yet be true to our beliefs that learning is a matter of growth and development; we want to hold students accountable yet be sensitive to legitimate needs; we want to alert students to error, yet reward what's done well.

I have my way of evaluating students' multigenre work, and I'll explain my method and rationale in this chapter. First, however, I direct you to these useful books whose authors discuss evaluation: Camille Allen's *The Multigenre Research Paper: Voice, Passion, and Discovery in Grades 4–6* (2001); Melinda Putz's *A Teacher's Guide to the Multigenre Research Project* (2006); Suzette Youngs and Diane Barone's *Writing Without Boundaries* (2007); and my first book about multigenre, *Blending Genre, Altering Style* (2000). Each author forthrightly takes on the topic of evaluation and grading. Regardless of the age of the students written about, I've learned from the authors' discussions.

I've taught writing a long time, beginning in 1970 with teenagers when I student taught in a new rural high school that consolidated four communities. My mentor teacher chaired the English department and had been largely responsible for creating the eleventh and twelfth grade curricula: semester courses in Shakespeare, contemporary world literature, speech, modern American literature, poetry, and Introductory Composition. It was the rare American public high school in 1970 that offered a class for learning to write that wasn't journalism or creative writing. In those years we didn't know much about teaching students writing as process. That paradigm shift, however, was underway. Teachers across the land were incrementally working such understanding into their classrooms.

We graded students' writing the way our writing had been graded in college. The professor commented here and there about errors of grammar, form, and content. If she knew what she were doing, she kept writers aloft by taking note of bright spots in the essays—deft rhetorical moves, surprising insights, engaging thinking. Like the professor, we arrived at what we deemed a suitable grade and placed it on the paper with a final comment. Student writing had been evaluated that way for years. We held our scoring guide in our heads.

When I joined a teacher education department in 1995, I came to know a powerful organization that seemed at once guardian of high standards and tyrannical gatekeeper and nitpicker: The National Council for the Accreditation of Teacher Education, NCATE (say "en-kate"), the only four-letter word I know with five letters. At Miami University, we sought national accreditation for our teacher education programs. Meeting NCATE standards was how we achieved that. One way NCATE determined the quality of our programs was by examining students' successful completion of key assessments we'd built into our courses. In my case, each key assessment was tied to a number of NCTE standards and measured by a rubric, something I'd never before used to evaluate student writing.

NCATE made a rubric writer of me. My two English methods courses contained eight key assessments. I had to create a rubric for each. Faculty weren't left untrained. We were given a book about rubrics, in which the author discussed rubric rationale, touted their fairness and accuracy, and laid out the do's and don't's of designing them. Three days before school began, we attended a retreat and began creating rubrics. The columns, categories, and descriptors were alien to me, this writing teacher of thirty-five years. I thought of e. e. cummings' "a world of made / is not a world of born." Writing had always felt like something born to me, something creative, living, malleable, stable only when it was published. And the best writing contained something almost ineffable. Writing informed but could also affect the emotions. To measure it then with an "assessment instrument," as the rubric was called, seemed clinical, sterile, patently wrong. As a girl once said when breaking up with me, "Something inside me says, 'No.'"

In *Rethinking Rubrics in Writing Assessment*, Maja Wilson sums up my felt sense:

> If you're anything like me, you have mixed feelings about rubrics. You've used them. In fact, sometimes you really like them. Still, you've picked up this book because something about rubrics violates your "deepest conviction about the complexities of the writing process" (Anson 1989) and you question your own use of rubrics: are they really all they're cracked up to be? (Wilson 2006, 2)

Still, my job required me to make rubrics and make them I did. Truth be told, I found myself thinking of rubric construction, unbidden. Time I'd spent in the precious realm of reverie was usurped by imagining categories and wording to describe levels of achievement. I didn't like that. One rubric I created was for a multigenre assignment. I read students' papers, measured them against the rubric, saw where it had gaps. I revised for next time, read more student papers, came to new realizations, revised again. Like Jennifer in the epigram, I wondered how some papers scored rave reviews on the rubric but hadn't knocked me on the seat of my pants. I also wondered how to reward students when they did things beyond the rubric, things I wish I'd asked for.

If the rubric was going to be of value to me and my students, if I was going to retain a shred of integrity with my friends who taught writing (as I turned to the dark side), the rubric I created had to reflect the values I'd developed over decades of teaching writing, over decades of reading the work of stalwarts in my two areas of content—teaching and writing: Ken Macrorie *and* Marge Piercy, Donald Graves *and* Michael Ondaatje, Peter Elbow *and* Barbara Kingsolver. And embodying both teaching and writing, Donald Murray, columnist-novelist-essayist-poet *and* brilliant theorist and scholar of writing. My rubric had to show students my values about writing, particularly, multigenre writing.

I valued good faith participation—hard, dedicated, risk-taking work.

I valued writing that sang on the page.

I valued voice—after all, I'd written a book about it (Romano 2004).

I valued students learning the craft of writing, essential skills like choosing topics well, focusing, elaborating, sharpening, and tightening language. I also valued deft touches like humor, metaphorical language, allusions, and sentences that sounded like good talk.

I created and refined my rubric, seeking to imbue it with those values. I divided the rubric in half: a holistic part that was my gut reaction to the paper as a reader who longed to be informed, moved, and carried away by the power of written words. To arrive at a holistic grade, I read the paper through without making a mark on the rubric, without any interruption of my reading. I relied upon my experience as a teacher, writer, and reader, on my judgment of the paper's demonstration of writing craft, on whether, as Emily Dickenson put it, I felt as though "the top of my head were taken off." Here is the first part of my rubric:

____ **Holistic impact of the paper**

116–120 Knocks readers off their feet, so informative and emotionally moving is the paper. Throughout there is evidence of original thinking, depth, insight, specificity of detail, delights of language. The multigenre paper is rife with excellent writing that includes attention to a pleasing visage of the page, action verbs, varied sentence length, effective word choice, skilled placement of payoff information, strong leads and endings, visual and other sensory imagery. Research is interesting, surprising, deftly and creatively incorporated into the paper.

112–115 An excellent, fulfilling paper

101–111 A good paper. The writer has made some of the solid moves mentioned above. Readers learn about the topic. While the paper isn't moving, its execution is competent, its research is good.

90–100 Paper is complete, but writing does not consistently employ those qualities of voice and craft that make writing strong and vivid. There is a feeling of middle of the road about it.

79–89 Not an adequate paper. The writing shows almost none of the skills mentioned above. Some pieces seem perfunctory, as if written hastily and never revised. Content shows little depth or insight. More telling than showing. Research is minimal.

78 and
Plummeting Underdeveloped in both number of genres and quality of writing. Writer has not taken seriously the disciplined, creative act of writing and the integrity of her own mind.

A colleague in reading education, an excellent analytical thinker who works hard to teach students to write well supported, clearly argued essays, read the holistic part of my rubric and shook his head. I imagined him thinking, "Tom, Tom, Tom. Too soft, too cuddly, too unrigorous." I understood his disappointment. But I stand by my values of what makes strong writing, about the writing world being large with many ways—in addition to argument—of coming to know and express. This holistic part of my rubric has provided me with a modicum of comfort in applying an instrument to the multigenre paper, this form of writing that is so generative of thought and language, so imaginative in its leaps of perception, so creative in its conception and construction.

In the second half of the rubric, I turned my attention to specific parts of the paper I wanted students to write. For fully realized papers they would have to write more genres than I required, but I knew their papers would be better if they included a strong final piece, a golden thread, a prose poem, free verse, flash fiction/nonfiction, and readable, interesting exposition. Writing these would stretch students in rhetorically healthy ways. They'd become stronger, more versatile writers. On the day students turn in their papers, they clip a rubric to it and direct my attention to page numbers and genre titles I've required and need to evaluate. There are twelve required parts that add up to 120 points, 10 points for each part, half the paper's grade. The break down of points reflects my grading scale. An *A*, for example, is 9.3–10, giving me some range in making judgments.

Required elements:

____ **Title**

9.3–10   Original, illustrative, surprising, piques readers' interest, may be something mysterious about it.

8.4–9.2 Serviceable and clear, good.

7.5–8.3 Simply names the topic (e.g., "A Multigenre Paper About Vampires" as sole title).

0   No title.

____ **Introduction/Preface/Dear Reader (Not necessarily the first piece after the title page)**

9.3–10   Piques readers' interest and provides pertinent information, sets reader up for reading what is ahead, something magical, provocative, or moving about it, maybe unconventional in being comprised of two or three pieces.

8.4–9.2 Informative, perhaps no-nonsense, not too brief or too long.

1–8.3   Provides little substantive information, doesn't compel readers to read on, may be overlong or too brief, nothing really enticing about it.

0   Missing.

____ **Unifying Element(s)/Repetend/Golden Thread (Name your unifying element(s) with page numbers)**

9.3–10   Connections between pieces are easily recognized, surprising, creative, moving.

8.7–9.2 Unifying element present, effective.

8   Unifying element present but not particularly effective or memorable.

0   Missing.

____ **Visage (Name the visual element(s) with page numbers)**

9.6–10   Appealing to the eyes: Spacing, type size, readability and appropriateness of font make readers speed along, concentrating on making meaning. Contains strong visual element(s) that accomplishes something words alone cannot.

(continued)

9.3–9.5	Not at all physically hard to read. Visual element(s) add meaning.
8.4–8.9	Not physically hard to read. Visual element(s) present but not particularly vivid or meaningful.
7.5–8.3	Some print may be hard to read. Visual element more a frill, maybe simply downloaded, copied, or pasted in, no meaningful payoff.
1–7.4	Writer seems to have paid little attention to reader's physical experience with reading the paper. Little or nothing appealing. May be difficult to read in parts. Visual element(s) may be missing.

____ **Copyediting**

10	Perfect. Rules broken are purposeful.
9.7	Contains few errors in grammar, punctuation, spelling.
8.4–9.2	Contains more than a few errors but meaning not seriously affected.
7.2–8.3	Contains enough errors to the point of distraction. Writer, perhaps, has not proofread well or does not have knowledge of grammar, usage, and spelling.
0–6.5	Frequent, repetitive errors, a copyediting disaster.

____ **Poetry in Contemporary Free Verse Style (Titles and page numbers)**

9.3–10	Contains sensory images, specific descriptive detail, attention to line length and possibly the space between lines, titled, precise word choice, syntax not choppy or fragmented, in most cases will read in perfectly grammatical, complete sentences.
8.4–9.2	May lack some elements above that would have made the poem stellar.
7.5–8.3	Few images. Choppy or fragmented syntax. Possibly abstractions.
6.6–7.4	Little or no imagery, little attention paid to word choice and other poetic elements. Perhaps wordy and relying on generalized emotions or clichés.
0	Absent.

(continued)

____ **Expository Piece: 250–350 Words (Name the expository piece and page number)**

9.3–10 The emphasis is on explanation/analysis/persuasion, not narrative or description (though these modes may be present to enhance the exposition). Vivid, interesting information. Adds insight and depth to multigenre paper, is well written with active verbs, specificity, and few wasted words.

8.4–9.2 Informative and clearly expository writing.

7.5–8.3 Clearly expository writing, though information not vital to effect of paper. Writing could be tightened and sharpened.

0–7 Writer does not have clear understanding of expository writing.

____ **Prose Poem (Name prose poem and page number)**

9.3–10 Short block of type, a paragraph or two, sensory images present, a situation rather than a plot, no attention paid to line length. Fresh, intense language. Payoff.

8.4–9.2 Short block of type, a paragraph or two. Language not particularly intense or sensory.

7.5–8.3 Written in generalities and abstractions, little that is specific or imagistic.

0 Absent.

____ **Flash Fiction/Nonfiction or Startling, Pointed Narrative Vignette (Name and page)**

9.3–10 A narrative (story), contains character(s) who yearn, tension. Auditory effects may be enhanced. Some mystery or surprise. Often there is unease present at the end, a sweet ambiguity. Clear, effective, even moving payoff.

8.4–9.2 Interesting, though writer might tell too much and show too little. Clear payoff.

7.5–8.3 Too brief, not developed or carried through. Payoff absent or ineffective.

0 Missing.

____ **Final Piece/Genre**

9.6–10 The last piece adds a resounding, final note to the multigenre paper. Leaves the reader with a deep understanding or feeling that appeals both emotionally and intellectually. It might solve a mystery woven through the multigenre paper. It lifts the reader, it lingers.

(continued)

8.4–9.5	The last piece is functional, lets reader know clearly that the multigenre paper is complete.
7–8.3	The last piece is over-long or unrewarding or anticlimactic.

_____ **Works Cited**

9.6–10	Complete (10–15 sources), a range of research is represented (books, articles, book reviews, websites, primary sources), sources listed in a consistent bibliographic style.
8.4–9.5	Range of sources not as deep and complete as would warrant a 10.
7.5–8.3	Brief (under five sources), perhaps bibliographic style inconsistent.
7	Indicates minimal research.
0–6.5	Indicates that research has not played significant part in the multigenre paper or that research has simply been plopped into the paper or attached.

_____ **Endnotes**

9.3–10	Each piece that needs a relevant note has one. Writer uses this rhetorical space to inform readers about a dimension of the piece they couldn't otherwise know, such as elaboration of a point, further research, or the process of creation. Within the text of the paper, a parenthetical alert or a raised number indicates that there is an endnote entry for the piece. There is a surprising, fulfilling quality to the note.
8.4–9.2	Endnotes are informative and thorough. Parenthetical alerts or raised numbers appear in text.
0–8.3	Endnotes that are needed are not provided. Questions are left in the reader's mind. Or notes are largely perfunctory, hurting the overall effect of the paper.

The multigenre paper is large and contains multitudes. The rubric helps me pay attention to its totality. The holistic portion allows me to open myself to what the paper is doing, to feel it, just as I want to feel other crafted writing I read. The required elements remind me to examine how well students executed specific skills, strategies, and genres I've taught. More importantly, I think, the rubric helps guide and organize students' work, reminding them of requirements and the qualities that often make them effective.

In *Rethinking Rubrics*, Maja Wilson offers this pragmatic philosophical stance:

> Grading policies should not only help students to engage in the hard work of writing but should also encourage us to become better teachers. Policies that focus on process require teachers to foster insight into the writing process and provide opportunities for students to engage in it—they require us to *teach writing* rather than simply assign, correct, and return essays. (Wilson 2006, 85–86)

Between assigning multigenre papers and grading them are weeks of instruction and writing. You've read about these in earlier chapters: finding topics, developing research designs, diving into research, producing writing each week, getting feedback from me, giving and getting feedback in peer response groups, experimenting with various genres in quickwrites, revision workshops, and a final reflection/self-assessment. Engaging in such processes has kept me a writing teacher, not just an assigner and grader. When I work mindfully, I am a better teacher. I pay attention to where students aren't meeting my expectations and where my expectations are unreasonable, where students have difficulty as well as where they soar, where I may have fallen short in my teaching. I avoid the trap Holden warned about in *The Catcher in the Rye*: "If you do something *too* good, then, after a while, if you don't watch it, you start showing off. And then you're not as good any more" (Salinger 1964, 126).

We teachers want to steer clear of complacency, beware of self-satisfaction. If laurels come, accept them, thank the laurel giver, move on with your work. For a time you can skate by on reputation for past excellence, but when you stop paying attention to detail, when you start relying on autopilot, the quality of your work will fall off, the passion you once had will turn phony. As a teacher, you won't be as good anymore.

Coda

Marina was a student in my methods class. She was Macedonian-American, had been raised in the Macedonian Eastern Orthodox Church. She had fallen in love with a Muslim man and converted to Islam. Marina was devout and, as she interpreted her faith, always appropriately dressed. Her mind was lively, her words forthright, her ideas about education progressive, her sense of humor intact and at-the-ready. She was sure of herself, yet open to new learning, unafraid of change, and capable of swift insights. She was going to be the kind of English teacher I wanted my granddaughters to spend an hour with each day.

Marina wrote a multigenre paper about her spiritual journey and decision to convert to Islam. The same semester Marina wrote this paper, America was in its second year of war in Iraq. That spring images of Abu Ghraib broke. The humiliation and torture of prisoners by American soldiers was graphically displayed in the media. Marina was sickened and outraged by what she saw.

I had read her paper and partially scored it with the rubric. Superb work from Marina, as usual, an excellent rendering of her journey and the unresolved tensions within her family. Part of her multigenre project was the creation of a video spurred by the revelations and images of Abu Ghraib. She had spent hours editing and laying down a soundtrack of Islamic prayers and songs. My computer wouldn't play the DVD she'd given me, so Marina came to my office with her laptop. Together, in the dim light, we watched the video. I remember it running long and thinking that if there had been more time, Marina would have gained distance from her work and embraced the principle of "less is more," cutting the length to gain power. What I remember more vividly, however, is how agonizingly affected I was by the counterpoint of sound and images. Marina's video brought home not only the shame of Abu Ghraib. It made me think of the entire debacle of Iraq, a war I thought never should have been fought, the violence, the terror, the terrible clash of cultures, the tens of thousands killed and wounded by then, the incomprehensible despair now a part of so many lives in both countries. Marina's passionate multigenre project drove deep into my soul.

When the video was done, I sat back, sobered and drained. I picked up that three-page rubric and crushed it into a ball.

"How do you expect me to grade that?" I said.

Marina was speechless, a look of academic horror on her face.

"You went way beyond my expectations." I tossed the paper ball into the trash can. "Your achievement, Marina, makes the rubric trivial."

I don't need another rubric for why I missed the mark. I'm OK with missing the mark, falling short, being "less than you expected" or "not quite enough" to meet the next point category. If you are so experienced, why did you forget the category in your rubric that deals with my honest effort in grappling with tough subjects that I can't quite comprehend? It was in my honest effort and good faith that I wrestled with the concepts, at times pinned for what felt like hours underneath the hard and merciless weight of big ideas. Take some advice from me, the novice. When dealing with issues as big as or bigger than my developing brain, leave room in your rubric to grade them. Matter of fact, try to *grade* them. What you see on paper is only half the time, effort, and struggle I put in to forming less than certain ideas that I'm truthfully still deciding upon. I had a time limit, a deadline, a cut-off date, and therefore had to halt my impending thoughts (which could have "added to the strength of my argument") in order to make the cut for the "on time" section in your R-U-B-R-I-C. I'm still figuring out the world, you know. If you're going to ask me questions about my process for doing so, the assumptions I have, or the conclusions I decide to make, please DO leave room for the *figuring out* part I mentioned, which consumed more time than you took to grade the words I managed to arrange in a somewhat organized way even though my brain is still ascatter and feeling mushy and confined and all I want to do is talk about it. (You want to "grade" something? How's that run-on sentence for ya?)

Maggie Bensch, college junior

WHAT TEACHERS DON'T KNOW CAN HURT STUDENTS. I'M NOT talking about what teachers don't know about subject matter, though ill-preparedness is certainly a detriment. I'm talking about what teachers don't know about students, about their ways of learning, their processes of working. I'm talking about what teachers don't know about how they might best help students. When I read students' multigenre papers, I know I'm going to learn, but I want to know more. I want to know what will remain invisible unless students tell me.

As students near the end of their multigenre projects, I ask them to complete a self-assessment that will move them to reflect upon their work and accomplishment. I want students to tell about those firm beliefs they've developed during the project. I also hope my prompts jolt them into sudden learning. Their self-assessment perceptions are often the most lasting learning. Students go beyond what the teacher wants to what matters to them. Through this self-assessment, I'll learn about students, and I'll learn about my teaching.

Sometimes I have given students the self-assessment on the day multigenre projects are due, and let them take ten to fifteen minutes to complete them. I get fuller responses, however, if I give students the self-assessment the week before so they can type them and have more time to reflect. This gives the self-assessment more weight. In fact, just now as I am writing, I've made a note to myself to give the self-assessment a place on the rubric so it takes on greater seriousness and can be attached to the multigenre paper. This will give proper respect to that "figuring out" part Maggie believes is critical to fair assessment.

Depending upon the dynamics and purpose of the class, I place from four to seven items on the self-assessment. I want to find out things, but I don't want it to be burdensome. I ask students to be specific and show why they say what they say. Below are items I've used in the past, along with my comments and the responses of students:

To have them judge the quality of their writing and let me see their values, I have asked students to

- Identify the strongest piece of writing in your multigenre paper and explain why it is.
- Identify the weakest piece and explain why it is.

Students might be reluctant to point out weakness. They are less reluctant to share this if they can explain why. Students know I believe in process. They know I think writing is work just as much as I believe in "trust the gush" and "faith and fearlessness." On one occasion, a student thought her weakest piece was one I thought her strongest, which I'd read as a draft weeks earlier. Kristin, however, cut that piece from her final paper. She decided, she wrote, that the poem about the boat Percy Shelly was in when he drowned steered readers away from the focus of her paper, Mary Shelly. Commendable editorial acumen that surprised and impressed me.

- What did you learn about writing in different genres as a way of inquiring into your topic and communicating what you know?

Students often write about what the experience was like writing certain genres for the first time. They have written about particular writing fears that have been allayed. They've written about a respect they've developed for a genre they had avoided (often free verse poetry). They've valued the risks multigenre required them to take. One writer pointed out a transforming part of multigenre:

Everything old became new again. Though I have worked with almost every genre we discussed, I was surprised by the energizing sense of discovery during the writing process. A poem enhances research. Flash fiction supplies context for statistics. Dialogue supports main ideas.

Rob Scully, teacher

When peer writing lessons and response groups have been a significant part of our work, I've asked questions to gain understanding into how students were affected by that and how they functioned as collaborators:

- How did you help other class members create their multigenre papers? Tell stories.
- How did others help you create your multigenre paper? Tell stories.

My favorite question, the one that often leads to the most insight for me and for students, is one I learned from Don Murray many years ago:

- What surprised you?

I sometimes refine the question:

- What surprised you about researching your multigenre project?
- What surprised you about creating genres for your paper?

Sometimes I smile at the revelations, as I did when Ashley wrote about how topic choice had influenced her: "I was surprised by my own creepiness. It was exciting to reread the book more closely and come up with ideas to use in my paper. I'm glad I chose *Dracula* instead of a beach book."

I've learned about a student's relationship with the research element of the paper: "I was surprised at how much information I researched that wasn't directly related to my topic," wrote John. "I found myself reading about the European Enlightenment among other things. I had to re-focus my efforts a lot."

Another student makes an admission and provides an example:

I'll admit, at first I wasn't crazy about the research portion of the assignment. I couldn't figure out how to synthesize my research with my own personal message and genres. However, I was surprised at how much the research influenced me. For example, I learned that Virginia Wolff did a prewriting exercise to get the tone and rhythm of *Make Lemonade*. I used the exercise as a genre in my paper to explore the character of Jolly.

Jaclyn Kamman, college junior

Some students have written about "flow," that optimal psychological experience that is gold, wherever it is we find it:

I was surprised by how absorbed I became. I needed to remind myself to also approach the project with the perspective of gaining an understanding of how to teach multigenre in my classroom, but that was hard. All I could focus on was my research and writing, it completely consumed me for two weeks. But I enjoyed that aspect of it, too. I love to work hard on things that are interesting to me.

Ali Vandenburgh, teacher

You won't find Ali's realization transformed into a Common Core Standard for research and writing, but isn't what Ali experienced what we hope our students will experience somewhere in their education? That they learn what it feels like to be consumed by something academic—intellect, emotion, and fulfillment becoming one. With its emphasis of personal topic choice and the chance to create and communicate in interesting, wide-ranging genres, multigenre offers students that chance.

I want to keep reminding myself how I can clear the way for students so they craft their voice while writing with passion, so I often ask,

- What was helpful in writing your paper?

Depending on what I learn, I keep doing what I'm doing, stop doing something that's not helping, or start doing something I hadn't thought of. "The in-class lessons," wrote Ashley, "even ones that produced writing I did not use in the end, really helped me to start thinking about what direction I wanted to take my paper in and what I thought I could do with it."

To keep them on track, I have students turn in weekly check-point pieces of writing, which enables me to give them ongoing feedback, too. They might or might not use these pieces in their final paper. I didn't always do this. I learned how useful it was from a multigenre friend at Brigham Young University, Sirpa Grierson (2002). In one self-assessment, a student echoed the importance of such a strategy, more important even than what I consider my strongest pedagogy these last forty years:

Being required to submit writing nearly every class forced me to write, which led to a multitude of ideas and, I think, more creative pieces. You responding to our individual genres was most helpful. It made us try new genres and bring in new pieces as well as allowed us feedback. The individual conferences are helpful, but I think handing in pieces made us more accountable to actually write and produce works in multiple genres, which was good.

Megan Solon, college sophomore

In one more effort to learn something about student work and how I can improve my teaching, I might ask students,

- Is there anything that could have made writing this paper easier?
- Could Romano have done anything to make your work more productive?

"Make the paper easier?" a wag once responded. "Don't assign it."

I sometimes ask students to look ahead, a question especially important for teachers and teachers-to-be in my methods courses:

- What is your advice to future students who will write multi-genre papers?

Get started early! Do not be overwhelmed by the magnitude or complexity of the assignment. Once you get started it is easier than you think. I started this paper almost immediately after it was assigned and this was the best thing I could have done. That way, on the day it was due I was not typing like a mad woman. I was able to complete it in a way that did not stress me out or leave me dissatisfied with my final creation.

Elyse Silverman, college junior

Another student wrote,

Research everything. You never know what you will find and what a powerful connection you can make with the book through seemingly trivial information. I made most of my connections with obvious aspects of *The Bell Jar*—depression, electroshock therapy, and the author—but it was the little things that made the most impact on me.

Kristine (nee Scanga) Cagwin, college junior

Stephanie Brtko gave this advice that applies to writing anything: "Have a friend who has not yet read your book read your lit-based multigenre paper. He or she will be able to tell you where you have left holes in your work, making your paper accessible to all readers."

And Jaclyn had this multiple advice:

The most important thing I would want students to know concerning multigenre papers is to let the imagination run free (not wild). It can be scary
writing a multigenre paper for the first time, especially if you do not consider yourself a strong writer. Students are not often given the chance
to play with language. Multigenre requires you to take on different perso-
nas and experiment with styles and visuals. It's also important to teach
the relationship between visuals and words. Students often place these
two concepts in separate categories, when really they complement each
other and can go hand in hand to create a really strong effect. I would
encourage students to recognize and experiment with this relationship.

Because I want to know about my students' struggles, I ask,

- What did you find difficult about writing your multigenre paper?

Students have written about writing various genres, overcoming
procrastination, spending the necessary time on their papers, and
discovering a golden thread. A few over the years have even written
about the difficulty of "getting the words right," as Hemingway said
in answer to the question of why he rewrote the ending of *A Farewell
to Arms* thirty-nine times. Some version of getting the words right, I'll
admit, is a rare response to this question. With six to seven classes each
semester, students develop a truncated writing process that gets papers
written but not always with the craft they are capable of. Nevertheless,
I persist in demonstrating how writing can be tinkered with, revised,
rewritten, how such engagement of the whole mind can be pleasurable, a good way, in fact, to spend part of our wild and precious lives.

Kelly, a senior, had chosen to write about her father's alcoholism
and early death when she was seventeen. She had this to say: "The
just-captured emotions in my paper are difficult for me to talk about
for a few minutes, let alone write about and edit for hours."

Kelly's observation makes me think of the late Ken Brewer, my
friend of fifteen years, who applauded others when they wrote about
"the tough stuff." And I think of the encounter between Robert Frost

and the academic who asked him a question that implied Frost had chosen a word only for expediency.

"You can't really suspect me of just putting *retreat* there because of the rhyme," said Frost.

The academic laughed nervously and said, "It's a hard question."

"Yeah, well," said Frost, "that's the way it oughta be."

I want to tell Kelly that when we write about topics deep in our psyches, we can grow. They may be topics we often shy away from since to touch them is painful, they represent such sadness, such regret, such missed opportunity. But by grappling with them, we can mature. We can gain strength through giving words to the pain, through crafting language around it. Such writing can be mentally and physically healthy for us and for our relationships. I gave Kelly's paper to a close friend, a former high school student of mine, now a psychologist and recovered alcoholic of twenty years. He cared about good writing, and I knew Kelly's experience as a young adult would be interesting to him.

"Not only a good paper," Mark wrote to me, "but an example of how the work can be useful in many ways."

The work is the writing. The writing can be healing. If that happens with one of my students, I want to know about it.

Dramatis Personae

ROGER RHETORIC, PLAY-BY-PLAY ANNOUNCER

FIONA FANCY, COLOR COMMENTATOR

SCENE 1: ANNOUNCERS' BOOTH HIGH ABOVE A FIELD OF PLAY, WHERE
AN IMPORTANT CONTEST IS ABOUT TO TAKE PLACE.

Roger: Welcome, fans of writing. This is Roger Rhetoric and
my partner, Fiona Fancy, reporting from the Crucible of
Composition, a lovely facility that hosts every writing
event imaginable. Today we have an important match
between two titans.

Fiona: This promises to be interesting, Roger, even though some
prognosticators believe the outcome will be lopsided.

Roger: In just a few minutes, Multigenre, just twenty-five years
old in the world of student writing, squares off against the
tag team combo of College and Career Readiness Anchor
Standards for Writing and Common Core State Standards
for English Language Arts.

Fiona: If it's all right with you, Roger, let's just refer to them as
"the Standards."

Roger: Good idea, Fiona, like the Standards themselves, their
mere nomenclature is formidable.

Fiona: The odds, we should note, are heavily against Multigenre.

Roger: And that's despite Multigenre's color, flare, and popularity
among many teachers—

Fiona: Almost a cult following, don't you think?

Roger: Some would say so, Fiona. The challenge Multigenre faces today is daunting. The Standards are backed by business interests, government agencies, and the big boys of expository school.

Fiona: In fairness to Multigenre, Roger, I must point out that although many consider him synonymous with Imagination, Creativity, and Narrative Thinking, he has never had a quarrel with Argument and Informative/Explanatory writing, both highly prized by business.

Roger: That's true, Fiona, but Multigenre often *seems* in opposition to them.

Fiona: *Seeming* is not *being*, Roger. Let's not forget our Shakespeare.

Roger: Point made. Let's take a close look at Multigenre's opponent. The Standards carry themselves with a formal, intimidating air. Many teachers—and all administrators—see them as unassailable, what with their detailed elucidation, apparent comprehensiveness, and appearance of reasonable inevitability.

Fiona: And don't forget their extensive appendices.

Roger: Right you are, Fiona. The Standards have three of them: A, B, and C.

Fiona: No doubt, Roger, the Standards are impressive, and some believe there is a distinct bias in them against creative writing.

Roger: Controversy surely surrounds the Standards, even though they hold sway in many states of this great nation.

Fiona: It has gotten to the point, Roger, that anyone who opposes the Standards is labeled.

Roger: Oh, I've heard those labels: soft, naïve.

Fiona: Anti-intellectual.

Roger: Lacking rigor.

Fiona: Ouch! No teacher wants that label. But don't forget the ultimate slur: subversive to the American Way.

Roger: Yes, those critical of the Standards are sometimes accused of inhibiting our country's progress and disadvantaging it in the global economy.

Fiona: You know, Roger, the literacy scholar Thomas Newkirk notes that for years now, going back deep into the twentieth century with the rise of the factory model of education, there has been, and I quote him here, "a growing trend in education that requires teachers to work in preestablished (invariably research-based) systems that sharply limit their capacity to make decisions about curriculum and students" (Newkirk 2009, 10).

Roger: I can always depend on you to do your homework, Fiona.

Fiona: I like to be prepared.

Roger: But we must remember that there's nothing inherently wrong with basing teaching on research.

Fiona: Come, come now, Roger. We both know that all research is not created equal.

Roger: That's true.

Fiona: We also know that it is not unheard of for powerful publishing companies to tout only the research that supports products they want to sell to schools, and—

Roger: Hold on, Fiona, looks like our match is about to start. The Standards versus Multigenre, that hybrid born of reason and emotion.

Fiona: Fact and imagination.

Roger: The merger of heart and mind.

Fiona: And what we must not forget, Roger, is that Multigenre hails directly from our literary heritage.

Roger: You can't get more American than that, Fiona.

Fiona: Like literature itself, Multigenre is diverse, inclusive, and expansive.

Roger: Thoughtful and poetic.

Fiona: Driving and colorful.

Roger: But right now, Fiona, Multigenre faces the challenge of his life.

32

What's Right and Wrong with the Standards for Writing

I DON'T THINK THE STANDARDS WILL DO IN MULTIGENRE. Teachers who discover the energy and motivating power of multigenre will continue to use it at every grade level, even though there will be plenty of interpretation about the Standards' strictures, even though school systems will be tempted to buy teacher-proof Common Core curricular materials, even though multigenre doesn't fit neatly into any of the "text types" the Standards mandate. Here's what teachers understand multigenre does for students that will make it hard to kill off:

- Students experience the exhilaration of conducting inquiry driven by a personal need to know and the opportunity to communicate in multiple genres.

- Students experience how creativity and imagination are vital components of thoughtful research.

- Students exercise multiple intelligences.

- Students practice skills of analysis and synthesis.

- Students learn to be expansive in their writing.

- Students practice and refine research skills and examine the credibility of sources.

- Students learn note taking, bibliographic formatting, and creation of informative endnotes.

- Students learn to write interesting exposition.

- Students practice skills of grammar, usage, punctuation, and spelling. In fact, because multigenre writing engenders such excitement, students may be more inclined to take care in correcting the mechanics of their papers.

- Students experience the synergy of sharing ideas and accomplishment with peers who have similar goals.

- Students experience agency as they shape and structure their papers and show what they know beyond teachers' expectations.

- Multigenre addresses a multitude of Common Core State Standards in English Language Arts and College and Career Readiness Anchor Standards in writing, reading, research, and language.

A Closer Look at the Standards for Writing

It's not that the Standards for writing are bad. There is something for everyone in them. I can't read the Standards without respecting the time, thought, and language craft expended in producing them. You soon see that the Standards "put particular emphasis on students' ability to write sound arguments on substantive topics and issues, as this ability is critical to college and career readiness" (National Governors Association, Appendix A, CCSS 2011b, 24). In fact, the text of the Standards itself is an argument proposing and defending a "vision of what it means to be a literate person in the twenty-first century" (National Governors Association, Introduction CCSS 2011a, 5). The problem is that the Standards' vision for writing is narrow, biased, and incomplete. Sometimes the Standards feel divorced from the reality of teaching. They who wrote them are dismissive of writing that is something other than exposition, though narrative is given a nod as a "text type." Below are three of the four areas of writing that the Standards specify students should understand and be able to do:

Production and Distribution of Writing

4. Produce clear and coherent writing in which the development, organization, and style are appropriate to task, purpose, and audience.

5. Develop and strengthen writing as needed by planning, revising, editing, rewriting, or trying a new approach.

6. Use technology, including the Internet, to produce and publish writing and to interact and collaborate with others.

Research to Build and Present Knowledge

7. Conduct short as well as more sustained research projects based on focused questions, demonstrating understanding of the subject under investigation.

8. Gather relevant information from multiple print and digital sources, assess the credibility and accuracy of each source, and integrate the information while avoiding plagiarism.

9. Draw evidence from literary or informational texts to support analysis, reflection, and research.

Range of Writing

10. Write routinely over extended time frames (time for research, reflection, and revision) and shorter time frames (a single sitting or a day or two) for a range of tasks, purposes, and audiences (National Governors Association, CCSS 2011a, 41).

There is much to like there (and nothing incompatible with multi-genre). I, too, want clarity and coherence. I exhort my college students to keep in mind—especially after writing is launched—their purpose and audience. I push students to experience the clarifying power of revision. We want students to grow ever more sophisticated in their use of technology, and to "write to be read," as Ken Macrorie put it (1976), to write writing that works with readers. And is anyone against students using research to build and present knowledge? I would add here, however, that number 9 leaves the door open for a steady writing diet of analytical essays about literature, a narrow subgenre that has been, to my mind, overused in English language arts classrooms. Even "Range of Writing" I don't object to. My idea of bliss is "extended time frames," several months, say, of daily writing on a book manuscript. I want students to develop similar stamina for big writing projects. And writing with facility, even in "a single sitting"? Who doesn't want the quality of email, text messages, and tweets to be clear and substantive? (OK, I've got my tongue in my cheek. The Standards probably have in mind writing under testing conditions.) In a side note, the Standards declare that students "must have the flexibility, concentration, and fluency to produce high-quality first-draft text under tight deadlines. . . ." (National Governors Association, CCSS 2011a, 41). A line from Shakespeare comes to mind: "'Tis a consummation devoutly to be wished."

These three areas of writing fit comfortably with multigenre.

My objection comes with the first category of the Standards for writing: "Text Types and Purposes," which, I believe, is shortsighted, exclusive, and biased against creativity. And creativity, regardless of the genre being written, is the heart of linguistic expression, that generative quality of language that makes extended thought possible, whether writing a poem, a position paper, or a grocery list. Here is the Standards' first category that I omitted earlier:

Text Types and Purposes*

1. Write arguments to support claims in an analysis of substantive topics or text using valid reasoning and relevant and sufficient evidence.

2. Write informative/explanatory texts to examine and convey complex ideas and information clearly and accurately through the effective selection, organization, and analysis of content.

3. Write narratives to develop real or imagined experiences or events using effective technique, well-chosen details and well-structured event sequences.

---

*These broad types of writing include many subgenres. See Appendix A for definitions of key writing types. (National Governors Association, CCSS 2011a, 41)

It is the third "text type" I object to: Narrative. And I say this as a writer who sees narrative as the heartbeat of his writing. But for the Standards to single out narrative to the exclusion of all other genres that are not argument or informative/explanatory . . . really? What about making sure students write poetry? And drama? What about making sure students try bending and breaking rules of standard writing as a way of communicating powerfully, as Virginia Wolf and e. e. cummings did, as contemporary creative nonfiction writers do? What about making sure that all students—those who will become accountants and lawyers, as well as those who will become artists—write creatively?

I followed the asterisk after "Text Types and Purposes" to Appendix A. There the Standards elaborated on narrative, pointing out that it "can be used for many purposes, such as to inform, instruct, persuade, or entertain. In English language arts, students produce narratives that take the form of creative fictional stories, memoirs, anecdotes, and autobiographies" (National Governors Association, Appendix A, CCSS 2011b, 23). Sound thinking, I believe, that links to another laudable assertion: "The Standards require that students be able to incorporate narrative elements effectively into arguments and informative/explanatory texts" (National Governors Association, CCSS 2011b, 65). For years I have argued—often in the face of dogged opposition—that story/anecdote/narrative has a natural place in expository writing as a way to draw readers in, illustrate claims, add imagery, and people our prose (a sure way to heighten readers' interest). The Standards' understanding of the power of narrative heartened me. And then I saw a shaded, boxed bit of language beside the discussion of narrative:

Creative Writing Beyond Narrative

The narrative category does not include all of the possible forms of creative writing, such as many types of poetry. The Standards leave the inclusion and evaluation of other such forms to teacher discretion. (National Governors Association, CCSS 2011b, Appendix A, 23)

At first blush that clarification seems inclusive of multiple genres in that big world mural of writing. At second blush, however, I see those two boxed sentences as placating and dismissive. The writers of the Standards simply do not value creative writing. They essentially remove from students' writing repertoire the stock in trade of English language arts classrooms—literature: fiction, poetry, drama, experimental writing, prose poems, flashes, meditations, prayers, stream of consciousness, and so much more.

"The inclusion and evaluation" of creative writing beyond narrative, the Standards leave to "teacher discretion." How magnanimous of the Standards. How trusting of teachers' expertise and judgment, since the Standards leave no other text type to teacher discretion. Students *must* write arguments, *must* write informative/explanatory pieces, *must* write narratives. Why is creative writing left to teacher discretion? I fear that many teachers will be so bedeviled by the pressure to teach argumentative writing—the text type likely to be called for on a standardized test—that they will neglect creative writing altogether. The Standards point out that narrative does not include "all the possible forms of creative writing." That seems an odd assertion. Who would expect narrative to be inclusive of all creative writing? Poetry doesn't have to be narrative. Neither do all subgenres and hybrids of creative writing. Rather, narrative is more properly sheltered under the text type of creative writing. My hunch, however, is that the Standards writers did not want creative writing given the status of "text type." That would give it too much legitimacy. The Standards writers want to omit creative writing without seeming to. So it appears in an appendix.

Some will argue that I'm making too much of this, that even though it is in an appendix, creative writing is still a part of the Standards. I can't argue against that. But I can point this out: By placing it in an appendix with a two-sentence, dismissive caveat, the Standards diminish creative writing, give it second-class status, sanction its neglect under the guise of leaving it to teacher discretion. In fact, the text type of narrative, which is the closest the Standards come to creative writing, is undermined by the Standards document itself. Appendix C is composed of samples of student writing that would meet the Standards. Nineteen pieces of writing are presented by seventh through twelfth graders. Eighteen of these samples are categorized as either argument or informative/explanatory. The one narrative was written by an eighth grader (National Governors Association, Appendix C, CCSS 2011c). Though implicit, the message is clear: teachers may slight narrative. The Standards sure have.

Why did the Standards writers do this? Was it that the world of creative writing is simply too vast, which the little box seems to indicate by noting "all the possible forms of creative writing"? Or are there other, more insidious reasons for marginalizing creative writing?

Is it a devaluing, even a dismissal, of imaginative thinking that Albert Einstein and Immanuel Kant so valued?

Is it to make English classrooms more like business and technical writing classrooms?

Is it an assault on cushy thinking that many believe creative writing represents, primarily, I think, because they have never experienced its rigors? (I can still hear a guidance counselor say to me when I was a young teacher nearly forty years ago, "How can you grade creative writing? It's whatever comes out, right? It's creative.")

Is it because the Standards writers thought that their argument touting expository writing would be stronger if they simply minimized creative writing, while appearing to respect its breadth and depth?

Whatever the reasons the Standards writers had for marginalizing creative writing, I resist. I'm with high school English teacher Judy Michaels, who wrote in response to demands that students be trained to write clearly and concisely, in the way business people want to read,

> Okay, clarity and concision are fine, but as a teacher of the art and craft of writing, I'd like to help produce not only future employees in the global economy but also imaginative friends, siblings, lovers, neighbors, grown sons and daughters, and parents of imaginative teenagers. (Michaels 2011, 7)

The Standards relegation of creative writing to second-class status is a slap to that "art and craft of writing." It's rotten guidance to English teachers, too: "By all means," it implies, "have students read creative writing produced over the centuries, but to ensure that students are college and career ready, it is unnecessary to have them engage in such writing themselves." The Standards do not value ways of thinking and knowing that creative writing offers, at least as far as students are concerned. Imagination? Trifling. Associative thinking? Of little importance. A poet's eye for detail? Come now.

The Standards want writing that's all head, no heart.

In *Holding on to Good Ideas in a Time of Bad Ones* (one of the most important books about literacy education in the last twenty-five years), Thomas Newkirk lays out the range of discourse he finds essential: expressive, informational, persuasive, literary (Newkirk 2009, 152). Newkirk's second and third categories align with the Standards, though instead of the word *argument*, he uses *persuasive*. Newkirk's fourth category—literary—beats and includes the Standards' text type of "narrative." I'm guessing the Standards writers wanted to avoid *literary*, a term that makes some people uncomfortable, since so many as adolescents were overmatched by classic, literary texts and may also have been bludgeoned with strict interpretations of them to the exclusion of their own budding powers of reader response. *Literary* might also suggest elitism and condescension, as in "literary snobs."

I have to say though, "Too bad if *literary* makes someone uncomfortable." The Standards tout the use of disciplinary-specific language. *Literary* is about as disciplinary-specific as we can get in English language arts. *Literary* encompasses everything from the limericks of Anonymous to the abstract expository prose of Ralph Waldo Emerson. I also prefer the word *literary* to *creative*. Say the words "creative writing" and you often encounter an immediate dichotomy: some people dismiss creative writing as fluff; others believe it is sacred, something reserved only for the most talented writers. Creativity is not exclusive to narrative, poetry, and drama. Every act of writing is an act of creativity with language as the creative medium.

Two Further Gaps in the Standards for Writing
Mentor Texts

In Robert Frost's "Mending Wall" two neighbors meet each spring to repair the stone wall between their properties, rebuilding it to eliminate the gaps that have appeared over the winter. The Standards for writing, I believe, could also use mending. Frost's narrator says:

> "'Before I built a wall I'd ask to know
> What I was walling in or walling out,
> And to whom I was like to give offense'" (Frost 1969, 34)

The Standards have sought to wall out creativity, imagination, and narrative ways of knowing. And they've offended many teachers, especially teachers like me who want literary writing to have the status of argument and informative/explanatory texts.

"Standard 9 stresses the importance of the writing-reading connection by requiring students to draw upon and write about evidence from literary and informational texts" (National Governors Association, CCSS 2011a, 8). I applaud the Standards for using the language of "writing-reading connection," but oh, what a narrow view of it the Standards advance, harnessing the writing-reading connection only in the service of gathering evidence for writing arguments. There are other, more fundamental, connections between writing and reading: Both are active processes of meaning making. Writers and readers choose topics, immerse themselves in language, reread for understanding, revise their thinking. Breadth and depth of reading usually make for stronger writers. And students who begin to think like writers, actively using elements of writing craft, become more appreciative readers.

The strongest writing-reading connection is perhaps the use of mentor texts to teach students about writing craft and text possibilities. Scott Fitzgerald finally began selling short stories to *The Saturday Evening Post* after he learned the kind of story structure the magazine preferred. This he discovered by outlining short stories published in the *Post*. I wrote my first free verse poem after immersion in Marge Piercy's work. Nowhere in the Standards for writing do I see mention of "mentor texts"—of students looking to see, for example, how Anne Lamott structures an essay and then trying that out in their own attempts, of writing persuasive commentaries patterned after the op-ed columns of Maureen Dowd or Charles Blow, of writing poems that use techniques of Mary Oliver, Ken Brewer, or Mekeel McBride. On the concept of mentor texts as models for student writing, the Standards are silent.

Expressive Writing

By not including Newkirk's first category in his range of discourse—*expressive*—the Standards reveal a second significant gap: a spurning of writing process. The Standards don't mention expressive writing, yet without it, there is little chance students will write vivid narratives, clear explanations, elegant arguments. Expressive writing is where we start when we pour forth first words, seeking to make meaning from fragmented, chaotic inner speech. Expressive writing is writing closest to our speaking voice, the seedbed from which all other writing grows. Expressive writing with all its stumbles, indiscretions, lucidity, and exuberance gets us to our essays, reports, poems, and stories. Look at our notebooks—expressive writing. Look at our letters—expressive writing. Look at our drafts—expressive writing. When we begin to write anything, often with much doubt about what we will produce, we must keep faith in expressive writing.

"The aim of the Standards is to articulate the fundamentals, not to set out an exhaustive list or set of restrictions that limits what can be taught beyond what is specified herein" (National Governors Association, CCSS 2011a, 6). If expressive writing is not fundamental to learning to write, nothing is. Expressive writing is an absolute basic skill for students to learn to produce routinely with faith and fearlessness so language can work its generative magic. That expressive writing is absent from the Standards reveals profound ignorance about how writing is created or a calculated omission.

I don't really know if Multigenre will win its big match at the Crucible of Composition. The Standards has certainly opened the door to the possibility that teachers—conscientious teachers who want to do right by their students—will exclude any kind of writing from the curriculum that isn't argument, informative/explanatory, and narrative (with even the slighting of narrative a possibility). I know that multigenre encompasses the Standards' "range of discourse" and much more.

Many of us became English teachers because we thrilled to the big world mural of literature. We loved the grand stories of good, evil, yearning, and redemption. We smiled at ornery limericks. We imagined characters strutting and fretting their time on stage. We memorized lines from poems that spoke our unarticulated feelings. And when we got our own classrooms, we opened those imaginative worlds to students. That meant not only having students read the visions of authors, but also writing their own visions. We knew they would grow as language users if we broadened their possibilities for expression, if they tried writing stories that mattered to them as well as lucid explanations, if they created the precise imagery of poetry as well as extended arguments, if they cut loose with expressive writing in notebooks, journals, and first drafts as well as polished writing they let go to readers.

Maybe Roger and Fiona are wrong-headed in attaching so much significance to the match between the Standards and Multigenre. Maybe there doesn't need to be a winner. It's harmony I'm after. Multigenre is large. It contains multitudes. Despite the biases and the gaps I see in the Standards from my perspective of forty-plus years teaching writing, they, too, are large. I hope teachers see that. And if they come to believe in multigenre writing, I hope teachers boldly step forth, exercise discretion, and teach what the Standards omit, thereby mending them.

YOUR LIFE IS MULTIGENRE. DON'T DENY IT. YOU AWAKE IN THE morn with a dream in your head composed of the stuff of your life: memory, everyday detail, your desires, fears, and regrets—all blended in bizarre narrative fiction. In the kitchen you are all about exposition as you follow a step-by-step procedure to make a perfect cup of coffee. You arrange flowers in a vase, paying attention to color, shape, and height, trusting your eye and feel for composition. During the day you perceive a striking image, an incongruity, a surprise; a piece of lucky talk blooms in your mind, the first line of a poem it could be, even though you don't consider yourself poetic. Later, amid a room full of people, although you are silent, your mind flames with a high-speed interior monolog. You re-imagine that contentious meeting the other day, replay the dialog exchange and suddenly think of a point and line of logic that support your argument. On your way to meet someone for the first time, you're struck by an interesting way to begin the conversation, a lead that will delight and put the person at ease. Those first words you imagine saying make you think of those final words you said to someone beloved whom you knew you'd never see again. You'd wanted to get those words—that last connection—right. You remember that time from long ago when you were misunderstood; you think of an endnote that would have clarified the circumstance. And those two grandgirls these past seven years . . . they have become a golden thread through the fabric of your life, joining the passion you feel for shaping language on the page and seeing teaching ideas in so much of your experience. Your life is not one unbroken expository monolog. It is multigenre, filled with color, diversity, impressions, interpretations, other voices, surprises, tastes, smells, textures, images, sounds, sudden insights, puzzlements—some revealed, some not. It makes sense that multigenre becomes part of your teaching and the repertoire of writing you make available to students.

* * *

Some years ago, I received an email from a teacher:

From: Laura Lavallee

To: Tom Romano

Subject: Multigenre Success!!!

Date: Fri, 13 Jan 2006 11:17:04-0500

Hi, Tom:

I just wanted to send you a quick note about the successes of the multigenre paper in my senior critical analysis class this semester. I think it's one of the best things I've done as a teacher. I couldn't believe the quality of work I got from these students.

First quarter, they wrote a multigenre paper on their fiction reading book. We just presented today multigenre papers from "the countryside of the soul." Wow! is all I can say. The topics ranged from Star Wars to the death of a parent. I actually had a student come up to me after class and thank me for assigning this, saying that she now understands her classmates much better. A student who hasn't done any work all semester not only did the paper, but told me that "it was actually fun." I am blown away right now. It's almost surreal. I shared with them my multigenre paper on my parents' marriage throughout the process. I felt awkward at times, giving them such a personal glimpse into my life, but I felt it brought me closer to all of them and allowed them to write about personal things as well. So I'm thanking you for passing this all on.

Take Care,

Laura LaVallee

Laura's astonishment and pedagogical joy are not uncommon for teachers who take the multigenre plunge. As with most ideas we try, this one takes trust. It was nearly two years after reading *The Collected Works of Billy the Kid* before I tried multigenre with a group of high school students. You can be fiercer of heart than I. You can be more like Laura. After experiencing multigenre writing herself one summer in a class I taught at the University of New Hampshire, she launched into the project once school began.

Multigenre appeals to me because of my literary tastes, writerly passions, and sense of responsibility as a writing teacher. I am driven, too, I know, by my own schooling that was for so many years bereft of multiple genres in my own writing. Since then, it's been a gas: poems, narratives, commentaries, articles, notes, postcards, books, dialogs, letters, descriptions, expository persuasions, the boundaries between them sometimes joyfully blurred. In a final self-analysis of her learning one semester an undergraduate gave me a glimpse into changes that had taken place in her:

> Before this semester, I never considered that I could be a writer. Writing was a flavorless experience for me before now. Cranking out analysis papers for teachers had become easy and routine, but the monotony had turned me off from any personal experimentation with writing. I did not see how writing could be fun and enjoyable when it came to academia. But I have gotten a taste of something hot and savory. Writing poetry, free-writes, personal responses, and a multigenre piece has awakened a dulled hungering.
>
> *Mary Hannah Sanders, college junior*

I know this awakened hunger Mary Hannah speaks of. I felt it afresh that summer creating *Fearless Writing*. Immersion in a big topic of personal importance was invigorating. I want students to experience how such passionate immersion combined with the possibility of multiple genres can awaken a boldness of expression in them. They can contribute to that big world mural of writing. They are not Johnny-One-Genres. Their confidence rises with their accomplishment.

"I am large," wrote Walt Whitman. "I contain multitudes." Through multigenre your students can enter the same territory that Whitman inhabited, creative, rigorous, fulfilling. Students' subjective experience melding research and creativity will arouse their interest and positively affect their attitude toward writing. It will affect your attitude toward teaching.

Ackerman, Jennifer. 2007. *Sex Sleep Eat Drink Dream: A Day in the Life of Your Body*. Boston: Houghton Mifflin.

Allen, Camille. 2001. *The Multigenre Research Paper: Voice, Passion, and Discovery in Grades 4–6*. Portsmouth, NH: Heinemann.

Animal Crackers. 1930. Screenplay by George S. Kaufman, Morrie Ryskind, Bert Kalmar, and Harry Ruby. Directed by Victor Heerman. Hollywood, CA: Paramount Pictures.

Anson, Chris, ed. 1989. *Writing and Response: Theory, Practice, and Research*. Urbana, IL: National Council of Teachers of English.

Barbieri, Maureen. 2007. "Poetry Arrives." In *Teaching the Neglected "R": Rethinking Writing Instruction in Secondary Classrooms*, edited by Thomas Newkirk and Richard Kent, 103–18. Portsmouth, NH: Heinemann.

Beasley, Sandra. 2009. "Unit of Measure." *Poetry* 114 (4; July/August): 276–77.

Braestrup, Kate. 2007. *There If You Need Me: A True Story*. New York: Little, Brown.

Brewer, Ken. 2007. *Whale Song: A Poet's Journey into Cancer*. Salt Lake City, UT: Dream Garden Press.

Burns, Ken. 1990. *The Civil War*. Written by Geoffrey C. Ward, Ric Burns, and Ken Burns. Walpole, NH: Florentine Films.

———. 1994. *Baseball*. Written by Geoffrey C. Ward and Ken Burns. Walpole, NH: Florentine Films.

———. 1999. *Not for Ourselves Alone: Elizabeth Cady Stanton and Susan B. Anthony*. Written by Geoffrey C. Ward. Walpole, NH: Florentine Films.

———. 2001a. *Jazz*. Written by Geoffrey C. Ward. Walpole, NH: Florentine Films.

———. 2001b. "Ken Burns on the Making of *Jazz*." Available at www.pbs.org/jazz/about/about_behind_the_scenes.htm.

———. 2004. *Unforgiveable Blackness: The Rise and Fall of Jack Johnson*. Written by Geoffrey C. Ward. Walpole, NH: Florentine Films.

Butler, Robert Olen. 2009. "A Short Short Theory." In *Field Guide to Writing Flash Fiction: Tips from Editors, Teachers, and Writers in the Field*, edited by Tara L. Masih, 102–104. Brookline, MA: Rose Metal Press.

Capote, Truman. 1965. *In Cold Blood*. New York: Random House.

Chinquee, Kim. 2009. "Flash Fiction, Prose Poetry, and Men Jumping out of Windows." In *Field Guide to Writing Flash Fiction: Tips from Editors, Teachers, and Writers in the Field*, edited by Tara L. Masih, 109–15. Brookline, MA: Rose Metal Press.

Chopin, Kate. 1899. *The Awakening*. Chicago: Herbert S. Stone and Co.

Cisneros, Sandra. 1991. *The House on Mango Street*. New York: Vintage Books.

Coyle, Daniel. 2009. *The Talent Code: Greatness Isn't Born It's Grown. Here's How*. New York: Bantam Dell.

Csikszentmihalyi, Mihaly. 1990. *Flow: The Psychology of Optimal Experience*. New York: Harper & Row.

Diener, Ed. 2001. "Satisfaction with Life Scale." UIUC Department of Psychology. University of Illinois at Urbana-Champaign. 28 Apr 2008. Available at www.tbims.org/combi/swls/index.html.

Dos Passos, John. 1996. *U.S.A.: The 42nd Parallel* (1930), *1919* (1932), *The Big Money* (1936). New York: Literary Classics of the United States.

Dunning, Stephen, and William Stafford. 1992. *Getting the Knack*. Urbana, IL: National Council of Teachers of English.

Elbow, Peter. 1990. *What Is English?* Urbana, IL: National Council of Teachers of English.

Ernst Da Silva, Karen. 1993. *Picturing Learning*. Portsmouth, NH: Heinemann.

Essley, Roger. 2008. *Visual Tools for Differentiating Reading & Writing Instruction*. New York: Scholastic.

Fader, Daniel N., and Elton B. McNeil. 1968. *Hooked on Books: Program & Proof*. New York: Berkley Publishing.

Frost, Robert. 1969. *The Poetry of Robert Frost*. New York: Holt, Rinehart, and Winston.

Gendler, J. Ruth. 1984. *The Book of Qualities*. Berkeley, CA: Turquoise Mountain.

Graves, Donald H. 1983. *Writing: Teachers & Children at Work*. Portsmouth, NH: Heinemann.

Grierson, Sirpa. 2002. "Exploring the Past Through Multigenre Writing." *Language Arts* 80 (1): 51–59.

Haley, Alex. 1976. *Roots*. New York: Bantam.

Hart, James D. 1965. *The Oxford Companion to American Literature*, Fourth edition. New York: Oxford University Press.

Heard, Georgia. 1989. *For the Good of the Earth and Sun*. Portsmouth, NH: Heinemann.

Hemingway, Ernest. 1935. *Green Hills of Africa*. New York: Charles Scribner's Sons.

Horan, Nancy. 2007. *Loving Frank*. New York: Random House.

Hubbard, Ruth Shagoury, and Brenda Miller Power. 1993. *The Art of Classroom Inquiry: A Handbook for Teacher-Researchers*. Portsmouth, NH: Heinemann.

Hurston, Zora Neale. [1937] 1998. *Their Eyes Were Watching God*. New York: HarperCollins.

The Jazz Singer. 1927. Written by Alfred A. Cohn and Jack Jarmuth. Directed by Alan Crosland. Hollywood, CA: Warner Brothers.

John-Steiner, Vera. 1985. *Notebooks of the Mind: Explorations of Thinking*. Albuquerque: University of New Mexico Press.

Johnston, Peter H. 2004. *Choice Words: How Our Language Affects Children's Learning*. Portland, ME: Stenhouse.

Kaplan, Justin. 1980. *Walt Whitman: A Life*. New York: Bantam.

Keillor, Garrison. 2011. *The Writer's Almanac* (November 9). Available at http://writersalmanac.publicradio.org/index.php?date=2011/11/09.

KET. 2004. "Workshop 5: Teaching Multigenre Writing." *Write in the Middle: A Workshop for Middle School Teachers*. Lexington, KY: The Kentucky Network.

Kingsolver, Barbara. 1995. *High Tide in Tucson: Essays from Now or Never*. New York: HarperCollins.

Koff, Clea. 2004. *The Bone Woman*. New York: Random House.

Kooser, Ted. 2004. *Delights & Shadows*. Port Townsend, WA: Copper Canyon Press.

Kunitz, Stanley, with Genine Lentine. 2007. *The Wild Braid: A Poet Reflects on a Century in the Garden*. New York: W. W. Norton.

Lamott, Anne. 1999. *Traveling Mercies: Some Thoughts on Faith*. New York: Random House.

———. 2005. *Plan B: Further Thoughts on Faith*. New York: Riverhead Books.

Lane, Barry. 2009. *Multigenre Man: Tom Romano Talks About Multigenre Writing*. Available at www.youtube.com/watch?v=lucLoTMXxoE.

Lee, Harper. 1960. *To Kill a Mockingbird*. New York: Popular Library.

Lehrer, Jonah. 2007. *Proust Was a Neuroscientist*. New York: Houghton Mifflin.

Lyon, George Ella. 1999. *Where I'm from, Where Poems Come From*. Spring, TX: Absey and Co.

Mack, Nancy. 2006. "Ethical Representations of Working Class Lives." *Pedagogy: Critical Approaches to Teaching Literature, Language, Composition, and Culture* 6 (1; Winter): 53–78.

Macrorie, Ken. 1976. *Writing to Be Read*, Revised second edition. Rochelle Park, NJ: Hayden Book.

Masih, Tara L., ed. 2009. *Field Guide to Writing Flash Fiction: Tips from Editors, Teachers, and Writers in the Field*. Brookline, MA: Rose Metal Press.

McBride, Mekeel. 2006. *Dog Star Delicatessen: New and Selected Poems, 1979–2006*. Pittsburgh: Carnegie Mellon University.

Melville, Herman. [1851] 1964. *Moby Dick*. New York: Holt, Rinehart, and Winston.

Michaels, Judith Rowe. 2011. *Catching Tigers in Red Weather: Imaginative Writing and Student Choice in High School*. Urbana, IL: National Council of Teachers of English.

Moffett, James. 1983. "On Essaying." In *fforum: Essays on Theory and Practice in the Teaching of Writing*, edited by Patricia L. Stock, 170–73. Upper Montclair, NJ: Boynton/Cook.

Moncur, Michael, ed. 2006 *The Quotations Page*. Available at www.quotationspage.com/quotes/ Albert_Einstein.

Murray, Donald M. 1964. *The Man Who Had Everything*. New York: New American Library.

———. 1990. *Shoptalk: Learning to Write with Writers*. Portsmouth, NH: Heinemann.

National Governors Association Center for Best Practices (NGA Center) and Council of Chief State School Officers (CCSSO). 2011a. *Common Core State Standards for English Language Arts & Literacy in History/Social Studies, Science and Technical Subjects*. Washington, DC: NGA Center and CCSSO.

———. 2011b. *Common Core State Standards for English Language Arts & Literacy in History/Social Studies, Science and Technical Subjects, Appendix A: Research Supporting Key Elements of the Standards Glossary of Key Terms*. Washington, DC: NGA Center and CCSSO.

———. 2011c. *Common Core State Standards for English Language Arts & Literacy in History/Social Studies, Science and Technical Subjects, Appendix C: Common Core Standards for ELA/Literacy: Samples of Student Writing*. Washington, DC: NGA Center and CCSSO.

Newkirk, Thomas. 2009. *Holding On to Good Ideas in a Time of Bad Ones: Six Literacy Principles Worth Fighting For*. Portsmouth, NH: Heinemann.

———. 2011. *The Art of Slow Reading: Six Time-Honored Practices for Engagement*. Portsmouth, NH: Heinemann.

O'Brien, Tim. 1990. *The Things They Carried*. New York: Penguin Books.

Oliver, Mary. 1992. *New and Selected Poems*. Boston: Beacon Press.

———. 1994. *A Poetry Handbook*. New York: Harcourt Brace.

———. 1995. *Blue Pastures*. New York: Harcourt Brace.

———. 2002. *What Do We Know*. Cambridge, MA: DaCapo Press.

———. 2004. *Long Life: Essays and Other Writings*. Cambridge, MA: DaCapo Press.

Ondaatje, Michael. [1970] 1996. *The Collected Works of Billy the Kid*. New York: Vintage Books.

On the Waterfront. 1954. Directed by Elia Kazan. Columbia Pictures.

Oppenheimer, Michael. 1992. "The Paring Knife." In *Flash Fiction: 72 Very Short Stories*, edited by James Thomas, Denise Thomas, and Tom Hazuka, 140–41. New York: W. W. Norton.

Phillips, Rodney. 1997. *The Hand of the Poet: Poems and Papers in Manuscript*. New York: Rizzoli.

Piercy, Marge. 1973. *To Be of Use*. Garden City, NY: Doubleday & Company.

Power, Thomas. 2010. *The Killing of Crazy Horse*. New York: Alfred A. Knopf.

Putz, Melinda. 2006. *A Teacher's Guide to the Multigenre Research Project: Everything You Need to Get Started*. Portsmouth, NH: Heinemann.

Rebecca. 1940. Written by Philip MacDonald, Michael Hogan, Joan Harrison, and Robert E. Sherwood. Directed by Alfred Hitchcock. Culver City, CA: Metro–Goldwyn–Meyer Studios.

Rief, Linda. 1998. *Vision & Voice: Extending the Literacy Spectrum*. Portsmouth, NH: Heinemann.

Romano, Tom. 1995. *Writing with Passion*. Portsmouth, NH: Heinemann.

———. 2000. *Blending Genre, Altering Style: Writing Multigenre Papers*. Portsmouth, NH: Heinemann.

———. 2004. *Crafting Authentic Voice*. Portsmouth, NH: Heinemann.

———. 2008. *Zigzag: A Life in Reading and Writing, Teaching and Learning*. Portsmouth, NH: Heinemann.

Salinger, J. D. 1964. *The Catcher in the Rye*. New York: Bantam Books. (Originally published 1951 by Little, Brown.)

Sandburg, Carl. 1950. "Jazz Fantasia." In *Complete Poems*. New York: Harcourt, Brace and Co.

Siporin, Ona. 1995. *Stories to Gather All Those Lost*. Logan, UT: Utah State University Press.

Stafford, William. 1986. *You Must Revise Your Life*. Ann Arbor: The University of Michigan Press.

———. 1993. *The Darkness Around Us Is Deep*. New York: HarperCollins.

Stoker, Bram. [1897] 1997. *Dracula*. New York: W. W. Norton and Company.

Thomas, James, Denise Thomas, and Tom Hazuka, eds. 1992. *Flash Fiction: 72 Very Short Stories*. New York: W. W. Norton.

Vonnegut, Kurt. 1969. *Slaughterhouse-Five*. New York: Dell.

Whitman, Walt. [1855] 1981. *Leaves of Grass*. Franklin Center, PA: The Franklin Library.

———. n.d. *Leaves of Grass*. New York: Heritage Press.

Wilson, Maja. 2006. *Rethinking Rubrics in Writing Assessment*. Portsmouth, NH: Heinemann.

Youngs, Suzette, and Diane Barone. 2007. *Writing Without Boundaries: What's Possible When Students Combine Genres*. Portsmouth, NH: Heinemann.

IN 2012 MY SUMMER TEACHING FELL THROUGH FOR THE FIRST time since 1987. That was a boon for my writing life. In early May I dived into *Fearless Writing*. Ahead of me were fourteen weeks free and clear. I settled into a companionable writing schedule:

1. Light breakfast and then at my writing desk before 6:00 a.m.
2. About 8:30 a break and cup of French pressed coffee
3. More writing work until 10:00 or 11:00
4. Exercise—usually swimming (where some of the best thinking occurred)
5. Lunch
6. More work in the afternoon, part of that time planning the next morning's writing

In three months, I missed only six days of that routine. It was bliss.

That's how the book got written, but there would be no book without others:

At least four times now over the last twenty-five years Tom Newkirk of the University of New Hampshire has said things to me that altered my thinking and my path. The latest was a casual question before he took a bite of an appetizer at the Heinemann Authors' Reception at the NCTE convention in 2011. Tom asked if I'd thought about writing a second edition of my first book about multigenre writing. "No," I said, "I'd never write a second edition. *Blending Genre* is a book of a specific time and place."

My wife told me my abruptness embarrassed her. But Tom had taken no offense, and he had planted a seed. The idea of a second book about multigenre began rising to my consciousness often over the next month. By Christmas I knew it would be my next project. Much thanks, Tom.

I've published books with Heinemann for more than a quarter century. This go-round, I thank Lesa Scott, Vicki Boyd, Roberta Lew,

Kim Cahill, Sarah Fournier, Hilary Zusman, Shawn Girsberger, and Adam Curtis. Tobey Antao has been my editor for *Fearless Writing*. In addition to saving me from gaffes, errors, and omissions, she has made suggestions I followed that led to a better book. The Heinemann team has given me the same cordiality, respect, and moxie I got in 1985 from Heinemann's first editor-in-chief, Philippa Stratton.

I thank the Ohio Writing Project at Miami University, the New Hampshire Literacy Institutes at the University of New Hampshire, and the Martha's Vineyard Summer Institute through Northeastern University. I taught summer writing workshops for these institutions, where I learned the possibilities multigenre held for teachers in both their writing and their pedagogy.

Over the years I have been friends with some impressive women. Two of them figured into the creation of *Fearless Writing*. Thanks to Linda Rief, language arts teacher at Oyster River Middle School in Durham, NH. A friend since 1985, Linda and her husband, George, provide me lodging when I teach at UNH. Twenty-seven years ago when she anonymously read the manuscript of my first book, Linda earned the title of "that woman." She risked that label again when she read a chapter of this book and gave me response that moved me to keep my inner eighth grader at bay. I thank Penny Kittle, who traded email with me throughout the summer, sharing good writing and bantering about craft, publishing, and teaching. Talk to Penny and you want to write. When I was in the presence of our mutual friend, Don Murray, I always thought I stood taller. I think that way about Penny, too. Maybe the most important thing Penny did for me during this project was to clothe me appropriately. Just about every morning at my writing desk I wore a white T-shirt with advice featured on the front in large typewriter font: "Shut up and write"—a gift from Penny I'd forgotten until I fished it out of a bottom drawer.

Even without my former students I'd have written a book, but I wouldn't, couldn't, have written this one. So many of my students over the years have showed me ways of thinking and saying that increased my wisdom as a teacher of writing. I'm grateful to former students who gave me permission to publish their words. I extend extra thanks to Jonathan Graham, Marina Rana, Ashley Szofer, and Carrie Stanek Ferrari. They helped me get details right.

I thank my niece, Vicki Bolton Cessna, for the terrific back cover photo of the grandgirls and me that she captured during a family weekend of stories, hubbub, and lobster. She has a photographic eye and a critical consciousness. She knows how to pull over to the side of the road and phone a radio talk show host to set him and his audience straight.

I thank Masha Stepanova, librarian extraordinaire, at Miami University's King Library. "You're fun to hunt for," she tells me. Theresa Williams, a graduate assistant in my department, tracked down bibliographic information and helped me prepare permission letters. Graduate assistant Alexandra Vikartofsky and undergraduate Megan Dincher gave me sound editorial advice. Sabina Foot, graduate secretary for the UNH English department, led me to former students I could not find. Sarah Zerwin, high school English teacher in Colorado and editor of *Statement*, sent me reviewers' feedback that drew me into important rethinking on one chapter.

From 2008 to 2012 I was one of two Naus Family Faculty Scholars at Miami University. This endowed professorship was made possible by the beneficence of Jim and Susan Naus, both Miami grads. Their generosity enabled me to purchase equipment and supplies, support my students' professional development, and cover my travel expenses. Thank you, Jim and Susan.

There are distant teachers and intellectual allies I want to acknowledge: Walt Whitman, Ernest Hemingway, Kurt Vonnegut, and Marge Piercy. They wrote in ways that made me—at various points in my life—want to emulate writing that is clear, subtle, accessible, and sometimes startling. All who want to write must find their own distant mentors. And these teacher-writers have been irreplaceable to my growth and understanding—Ken Macrorie, Peter Elbow, Kim Stafford, and Anne Lamott. With keen perception, humor, surprise, and urgent voices they told truths I often felt in my bones but had not articulated.

If you felt a third presence in addition to you and me as you read *Fearless Writing*, I wouldn't be surprised. Around me as I wrote were the spirits of Don Murray, Ken Brewer, and Don Graves. The Dons were colleagues at the University of New Hampshire and my former teachers and friends since 1984. Ken Brewer was a poet and kindred spirit since 1991 at Utah State University. Ken's influence made me a better teacher, a better writer, a better man. My talk over the years with Murray, Graves, and Brewer was often about writing. They exceeded the standard that's my bottom line for writing teachers. When I left them, I always wanted to write more.

I thank my daughter, Mariana Romano, English teacher at Evanston Township High School in Illinois. For more than four decades this smart, funny, savvy child-teen-woman-wife-mother has been in my life. Mariana talked multigenre with me aplenty, sharing assignments, teaching strategies, and student papers. She's been part of every book I've written.

Lastly, I thank Kathy, my long time friend, partner, helpmate, lover. We are a mean team in the kitchen. Kathy clears the way for me to write with passion and craft my voice. During the summer of fearless writing, she took over the bulk of cooking, life organization, and care of our wire-haired fox terrier who, right now, is curled up on the rocking chair beside me, dozing. His name is Whitman.